Religion and State in Israel

Law and Religion

Volumes published in this Brill Research Perspectives title are listed at *brill.com/rplrs*

Religion and State in Israel

Past and Future Challenges

By

Gideon Sapir

BRILL | NIJHOFF

LEIDEN | BOSTON

The Library of Congress Cataloging-in-Publication Data is available online at https://catalog.loc.gov

Typeface for the Latin, Greek, and Cyrillic scripts: "Brill". See and download: brill.com/brill-typeface.

ISSN 2468-2985
ISBN 978-90-04-75887-2 (paperback)
ISBN 978-90-04-75888-9 (e-book)
DOI 10.1163/9789004758889

This book is printed on acid-free paper and produced in a sustainable manner.

Religion and State in Israel

Past and Future Challenges

By

Gideon Sapir

BRILL | NIJHOFF

LEIDEN | BOSTON

The Library of Congress Cataloging-in-Publication Data is available online at https://catalog.loc.gov

Typeface for the Latin, Greek, and Cyrillic scripts: "Brill". See and download: brill.com/brill-typeface.

ISSN 2468-2985
ISBN 978-90-04-75887-2 (paperback)
ISBN 978-90-04-75888-9 (e-book)
DOI 10.1163/9789004758889

This book is printed on acid-free paper and produced in a sustainable manner.

Contents

Introduction

The purpose of this essay is to present the challenges in the field of religion-state relations that the State of Israel currently faces.

Ostensibly, it could be argued that Israel's challenges in this area are pre-dictated, considering the state's definition in its basic documents as a "Jewish and democratic state." However, this definition does not mean much. On the one hand, the terms "Jewish" and "democratic" can be filled with a wide variety of meanings, leaving a wide range of possibilities regarding the shaping of the character of the state. On the other hand, if we adopt an "end version" for each of the terms, the connection between them will become an oxymoron. Some will argue that the fact that Israel is a Jewish state requires a close tie between the state and the Jewish religion. Others will argue that Israel's being a democracy requires the privatization of religion, while separating it from the state. However, these two positions are not only incompatible with each other, they are also far from convincing in themselves.

Indeed, throughout most of the years of the Jewish existence, there was a close connection between its national and religious foundations, but in recent centuries this connection has been challenged. Some abolished the national component, while others freed themselves from their commitment to the religious component. Accordingly, the definition of Israel as a Jewish state is open to a variety of possibilities, some that would emphasize the national element, some that would emphasize the religious element, and some that would deny both, and load the term "Jewish" in the definition of the state with a "thin" meaning, which would include only the fact (or requirement) that the majority of the country's citizens are (or should continue to be) Jewish.

Similar things can be said regarding Israel's definition as a democratic state. First, like the term "Jewish," the term "democratic" can also be interpreted narrowly and broadly. Defining Israel as democratic negates the possibility of turning it into a theocracy – but it still leaves a wide range of possibilities, and separation is only one of them. Even commitment to the liberal tradition does not require the adoption of the model of separation.

Supporters of Separation in Israel often rely on what they see as the American model, that of a "Wall of Separation." This wall is thought to be anchored in the First Amendment, which states: "Congress shall make no law respecting an establishment of religion or prohibiting the free exercise thereof." But this reliance ignores the complexity of American legal history. For about a century, the amendment was applied only to the federal government, not to the states

 | DOI:10.1163/9789004758889_002

most of whom maintained a tight connection with Christianity, as embodied in religious laws and in the specification of Christianity as the state religion.

After the Civil War, the prohibition on the establishment of religion was extended to the states, but even then, it did not occur to anyone to suggest absolute separation between state and religion, on either the federal or the state level. On the contrary, everyone believed that the nation's religious, or, more precisely, Christian character was an essential part of American identity. It took 150 years before the metaphor "Wall of Separation" was adopted by Justice Hugo Black of the Supreme Court, in 1947, and even then, there was no general agreement about its meaning.

When we turn to Europe, support for Separation is even weaker. The European Union explicitly recognizes the right of its member states to establish a religion, not only in the sense of supporting it, but in the sense of the explicit adoption of a particular religion as the state religion. Various forms of established religion were developed in Eastern Europe in most of the states that had been part of the Soviet Union, and to date state religions are the norm rather than the exception in Europe.

The fact that most liberal countries – and, a fortiori, illiberal ones – permit some kind of establishment of religion does not in itself mean that all the arrangements that are practiced in Israel today are legitimate, and later on, I will point out a number of arrangements that need to be changed – for example, in the area of personal status (marriage and divorce) and public transportation on the Sabbath.

One of the main arguments that will be presented in this essay is that in recent years, the map of challenges in the field of religion-state relations has in Israel largely changed its face. The demographic reality in Israel is changing – the ultra-orthodox sector is growing, as is its relative share in the population. This fact presents us with new dilemmas and intensifies old dilemmas that in the past could be pushed aside. As a result, the current main challenge that Israel faces in the field of religion-state relations is finding a way to integrate the ultra-orthodox sector into the various circles of life.

Our natural inclination is to deal with the "here and now," while ignoring the past. This is a mistake! The examination of the past is of great value, not only for historians, but also for those who wish to deal with current questions. This essay will therefore include not only a description and assessment of the current situation, but also a concise overview of the relevant history, from the beginning of Zionism, in the mid-19th century, to the present day. The less patient reader may prefer to skip part of the review and go directly to the chapters dealing with the current situation. This is a legitimate choice, but in order to reduce this "danger," I will briefly point out two important insights that I will extract from studying the historical chapters.

Many point out that in various matters in the field of religion-state relations in Israel, there is a significant gap between the law in the book and the law on the ground. A historical review will show that such a gap characterized the field from its inception, long before the establishment of the state. This fact is likely to sharpen awareness of the limitations of legal regulation, and accordingly it may weaken the religious motivation to use legislative tools to adapt the reality to the religious instructions. At the same time, a review of history may cool the motivation of some of the Israeli public to put its faith in the court, and to hope that it will bring about necessary changes.

As is well known, although Israel is a Jewish state, it has a significant minority of citizens of another religion. An exhaustive discussion of the challenges in the field of religion and state therefore requires discussing the status of the other religions in Israel and of the citizens who belong to them. Nevertheless, this essay will not deal with the subject, for the following reason: Unlike many countries where matters of religion and state can be separated from questions relating to national identity, in Israel, the question of the state's relations with its minority religions is intrinsically connected to the question of the national status of these minority groups. Dealing with the latter question through the prism of nationalism would have gone beyond the boundaries of this work, whereas an attempt to examine the question only through the usual prism of religion-state relations would have obscured the "real" dilemmas.

The structure of the essay is as follows:

The first chapter is divided into two sections. The first part will focus on the period from the middle of the 19th century to its end. In this section, I will describe the background and factors that led to the Jewish national revival in the Diaspora. Like the national awakening around the world, which was influenced, among other things, by the decline of religion, in the Jewish case, too, the crisis of religion contributed to the strengthening of national sentiment, either as a substitute for the lost religious identity or as a means of helping to strengthen the ranks of religion. During this period, there was a general agreement that Jewish settlement in the Land of Israel would be committed to the traditional way of life, but as the new settlement took shape, disagreements over the place of religion arose. The second part of the chapter will cover the period between the beginning of the 20th century and the establishment of the state in 1948. With the development of the Zionist enterprise, the question of the place of religion became more practical. The dispute over questions of religion and state took place in two arenas: in the Zionist institutions and in the developing settlements. Deliberations in both avenues led to a similar result: while the religious did succeed, to some extent, in influencing the decisions made on religious matters, these decisions had little impact on the situation on the ground.

The second chapter will focus on the period between the establishment of the State and the political upheaval that took place in 1977. During these years, matters of religion and state in Israel were regulated under the principle of the status quo, and enjoyed a great deal of stability. At the beginning of the chapter, I will examine when exactly the status quo was created and what were the powers that pushed for its creation. Then I will point to two main factors that contributed to the resilience of the status quo: political stability, which was expressed in a "historic alliance" between the dominant ruling party, the Labor, and the national-religious party, and the fact that during these years the Supreme Court rarely intervened in matters of religion and state. I will qualify the latter insight somewhat, and point out that even during this period, the court did intervene, from time to time, in arrangements that it considered particularly problematic.

The third chapter will describe the situation in the period between the "political upheaval" in 1977 and the end of the 20th century. This period was characterized by two phenomena. The first is the gradual erosion of the status quo, due to two main factors: the changes that have taken place in the political map, in which the left has lost primacy, but the right has not gained full hegemony, and the change in the Supreme Court's attitude to controversial issues. The change in the balance of power abolished old loyalties, opened the political field to negotiations, and strengthened the bargaining power of the religious camp. The Supreme Court's increasing interference in matters of religion and state has undermined old arrangements and made it difficult to formulate new agreements. The second phenomenon is the awakening of the public discourse on matters of religion and state, due to two factors: the need to examine and shape the components of shared identity, against the background of the collapse of the old components of identity, and the social rift between the right and the left, which has intensified, causing many to look for ways to bring hearts together.

The fourth chapter will focus on the period between the beginning of the 21st century and the present day. This period is characterized by two processes: the secularization of the public sphere and the change in the focus of disagreement on matters of religion and state. Even before the establishment of the State, the field of religion-state relations was characterized by a gap between the law in the book and the law on the ground. In recent decades, this gap

has been widening as many arrangements are not enforced in practice. This is despite the fact that at the same time there is a noticeable trend of getting closer to tradition. I will offer two complementary explanations for this phenomenon: the strengthening of the consumer culture alongside the weakening of the religious parties' interest in enforcing the arrangements in these matters.

The second process, i.e. the change in focus, is reflected in the decline in the importance of issues that previously preoccupied the political system and the emergence of new dilemmas, mainly relating to the state's relations with the ultra-orthodox public. The decline in the centrality of the long-standing disputes stems, inter alia, from the fact that some of them have found solutions that bypass the law, and others have been resolved through the failure to enforce the law. The emerging focus on the relations between the state and ultra-orthodox society stems from the significant increase in that sector's relative share. The expansion of the ultra-orthodox sector makes some of the existing arrangements problematic and creates new points of friction between the ultra-orthodox sector and the general public.

The fifth chapter will describe the developments on several key issues relating to the relations between the state and the ultra-orthodoxy – a description that will help us understand the dilemmas and challenges in this area. The chapter will briefly touch on another emerging challenge, related to Israel's immigration policy, which has led to the creation of a group of immigrants that does not belong to the Jewish collective. This challenge does not directly relate to the relationship between religion and state, but rather to the question of the national identity of the state. However, certain aspects of the issue have been included in the discussion of religion and state in the past, so I have chosen to address it briefly.

The sixth and final chapter will discuss ways to deal with these challenges. It outlines the general boundaries within which the various arrangements should be placed, as well as appropriate political tools and moods that will improve the chances of reaching a practical and fair settlement.

CHAPTER 1

From the Beginning of Zionism to the Establishment of the State

1 The First Jubilee – from the Middle to the End of the 19th Century

The First Zionist Congress was held in 1897, but Zionist activity began in the middle of the 19th century. The awakening of nationalism in the Jewish context was largely influenced by the general trend in the world during this period. There is a scholarly disagreement as to whether nationalism is an "ancient" phenomenon or whether it is a modern one,[1] but even those who believe that national consciousness is an ancient phenomenon will agree that during the 19th century there was a national awakening throughout the world.

In his book, "Parallels Meet," Ehud Luz describes the background to the formation of the Jewish national movement in the modern era.[2] During the 19th century, the Jewish community in Eastern Europe, in an area known as the "Zone of Settlement," experienced a severe social and economic crisis, which led to the collapse of the Old World order, including the weakening of religious commitment. Some of the young people of the community completely abandoned their Jewish heritage and assimilated, but alongside them was also a thin layer of intellectuals, who refused to give up their Jewish identity. Those intellectuals, who no longer found their place in the religious community, found themselves in a deep spiritual-identity crisis. The idea of national revival provided these intellectuals with a way out of the crisis, and it became an alternative identity anchor for them. They quickly translated the personal solution they found into a general manifesto, according to which the idea of national revival was the only one that could unite all the factions of the Jewish people.

As Luz points out, the nascent national movement was joined by two other groups. One group consisted of orthodox rabbis, who were aware of the religious crisis and were looking for ways to deal with it. They believed that the idea of national revival and activism for the Land of Israel would bring blood

1 For the modernist approach, see, for example, Ernst Gellner, Nationalities and Nationalism (1983); for the primordial approach, see, for example, Adrian Hastings, The Construction of Nationhood: Ethnicity, Religion and Nationalism (1997).

2 Ehud Luz, Parallels meet: religion and nationalism in the early Zionist movement (Lenn J. Schramm trans., 1988).

 | DOI:10.1163/9789004758889_003

to the whitewashed veins of Jewish society, and provide the necessary energy to deal with the phenomenon of secularization. The second group included Orthodox intellectuals, who agreed that Jewish society must change in order to adapt it to modern reality, but unlike their secular allies, they remained loyal to the dictates of Halachah. Their joining the creation of a national movement stemmed from the hope that the settlement of the Land of Israel would provide an infrastructure that would enable the construction of a synthesis between religion and the demands of the modern Enlightenment.

From the above description, it follows that the "forerunners of Zionism" (as the members of these groups are commonly denoted) acted for different motives. However, they all had two issues in common: the struggle against the anti-national spirits of Judaism (which came from the direction of Jews who integrated into European countries following the emancipation) and the understanding that religion plays a significant role in promoting the idea of national revival. Some of them saw the nation as the servant of religion, and others saw religion as the servant of the nation. But everyone understood that religion had a role to play.

In the early 1880s, the activities of the forerunners of Zionism began to take shape. In 1884, a conference of Hovevei Zion, the umbrella organization that coordinated Zionist activity, was held in Katowice. The gathering under one roof raised a dispute over who would lead the movement, but as Yosef Salmon points out, it was more of a power struggle than a struggle over contemporary content. On the content level, there was a general agreement that Jewish settlement in the Land of Israel would be committed to the traditional way of life.[3] The vast majority of the immigrants in the First wave of immigration had families and were observant. The only notable exception was the Bilu movement (Beit Yaakov Lechu Ve-Nelcha), a group of several dozen young people who established the village of Gedera. Although these young people removed their religious morals, they too committed themselves to observing the commandments in public, as evidenced by the magnificent synagogue building (in terms of those days) that still stands today on the main street of the (now) city.

Over time, and as the new settlement took shape, tensions began to erupt between the utopias – those of the religious and those of the secular. An example of the growing tensions was the controversy that arose between 1894 and 1896 over the initiative to establish a school in Jaffa.[4] One of the central

---

3 Yosef Shalmon, *Religion and Nationalism in the Early Zionist Movement, in* Jewish Nationalism and Politics : New Perspectives 115, 121 (Yehuda Reinharz, Yosef Salmon & Gideon Shimoni eds., 1996). [hereinafter Salmon *Religion and Nationalism*].

4 For more information, see, *id.* at 173–251.

figures in the Hovevei Zion movement was Asher Ginzburg, known by his pseudonym, Ahad Ha'am. Ahad Ha'am headed an organization called Bnei Moshe, which initiated the establishment of a new school in the city of Jaffa, as part of the idea that the cultural revival of the Jewish people must precede the political revival. The question on the agenda was in what spirit they would be educated in the new institution.

The question of the place of religion continued to occupy the National Revival Movement in its next incarnation, within the framework of the Zionist movement. The First Zionist Congress, which symbolizes the establishment of the Zionist movement, was held in Basel in 1897, and from the very first days of the movement, its leader, Theodor Herzl, was required to address the question of the place of religion, considering the controversy that arose on the matter. Several options were on the agenda. One possibility, which was rejected, was to turn the Zionist movement into a purely political one. One that would deal only with settlement and diplomacy. Another possibility, which was also rejected, was to give the observant Jews the right of veto over halakhic-educational matters.[5] Herzl himself, who was a secular man with Western liberal views, supported the reduction of the influence of religion on the governmental-public sphere. In this regard, the comparison he made between the army officers and the religious leaders is well known, when he proposed to "imprison" each of the groups in its compound – the military personnel in their barracks and the clergy in the synagogues.[6]

However, Herzl, who was a pragmatic man, was well aware of the contribution of religious sentiment to Zion as well as the fact that the majority of the public available for aliyah and contribution to the Zionist enterprise was observant. Therefore, Herzl expressed a willingness to compromise, including, for example, the establishment of a committee of rabbis to serve alongside the Zionist General Council, as demanded by Eastern European rabbis at the Second Zionist Congress. However, under pressure from vociferous and radical young people from Russia, who opposed any compromise, Herzl eventually retracted the compromise proposals.

With the expansion of the Zionist movement's activity, anti-Zionist movements also began to form among Eastern European Jewry. There were those

---

5 See, Yosef Shalmon, *The Struggle over the public opinion of the haredi community in eastern Europe concerning Jewish nationalism, 1894–1896*, in Studies in the History of Jewish Society in the Middle Ages and the Modern Period Presented to Professor Jacob Katz on this Seventy-Fifth Birthday by his Students and Friends 350, 364 (Immanuel Etkes & Yosef Salmon eds,. 1980).

6 Theodor Herzl, A Jewish State 38 (Jacob de Haas trans., 3rd ed. 1917).

who opposed Zionism for ideological reasons (the Bund).[7] But for our purposes, we will deal here with the objection that stemmed from religious reasons. The religious opposition was based on two pillars: halakhic and practical. The halakhic argument against Zionism was based on the prohibition of taking the initiative to renew Jewish independence in the Land of Israel. According to the argument, such behavior is considered to be pushing forcibly the end of exile and rebelling against the nations, actions that are explicitly forbidden by the Gemara.[8] As Avi Ravitzky explains, this opposition coincided with the view that the redemption would take place miraculously, as if the Third Temple was supposed to descend from heaven.[9] The practical argument was based on the reality that was emerging before the eyes of the rabbis. As Shalmon notes, "Even if joining the [Zionist] movement was not contingent on the participant's willingness to accept a secular identity, and the definition of Jewish nationalism was not secular in its content, there were still many who, by joining the movement, shed their identity as observant of Halacha. For many young people, the movement served as a transit station from the world of halachic observance to a "free" world. This was the ultra-orthodox argument against Zionism, as formulated by Rabbi Eliezer Gordon of Telz, one of the greatest rabbis of Russia at the time, that more than it 'purifies the impure, it defiles the pure.'"[10]

Although the secular nature of the Zionist movement distanced some of the observant public from it, religious leaders continued to operate within it. In 1902, the Mizrachi movement was founded, headed by Rabbi Yitzchak Yaacov Reines. According to Shalmon, the decision made at the Fifth Zionist Congress, according to which the Zionist Organization would also engage in cultural activities, was the main motivation for the establishment of the Mizrachi movement. The majority that was forming in the Zionist movement was secular, and accordingly, the content of the cultural activity was expected to serve in tension with the traditional outlook. Mizrahi's efforts failed in reversing the aforementioned decision, but in the end a compromise was reached, according to which "educational activity in the National Organization will be carried out separately by each of the dissenting parties, provided that it does not become part of the general Zionist program."[11]

7 For an overview, see, Yossef Gorny, Merging Alternatives: The Bund and Zionist Labor Movement, 1897–1985 (2005).

8 Babylonian Talmud, Ketubot 111a.

9 Aviezer Ravitzky, Messianism, Zionism, and Jewish Religious Radicalism (Michael Swirsky & Jonathan Chipman trans., 1996).

10 Salmon *Religion and Nationalism*, *supra* note 3, at 118.

11 *Id.* next to note 72.

From then on, the Mizrachi movement occupied a central place in Zionist activity. It represented the Orthodox position at the Zionist Congresses and made efforts, with little success, to shape Zionist activity in the spirit of old faith.

Already at this stage, as Ravitzky explains, it was possible to discern two different approaches among religious Zionists. One approach, whose main representative was Rabbi Avraham Yitzchak HaCohen Kook, saw the national revival as an expression of the redemption of Israel. According to this approach, the redemption is not a single event, but rather a process: the partial realization is not portrayed as the breaking of the whole, but rather as a continuous link in its development. In his writing, Rav Kook proposed a distinction between two stages in the process of redemption: The first stage, the stage of "Mashiach ben Yosef," prepares the ground for the second stage, the stage of "Mashiach ben David." According to this explanation, Zionist activity belongs to the first stage, the stage of the "initiation of redemption," and it does not replace the Final Redemption, but rather precedes it. This explanation could be reconciled with the secular nature of Zionist activity.

According to a second approach, whose most prominent representative was Rabbi Reines, the Zionist enterprise has nothing to do with redemption, and its only purpose is to improve the situation of our unfortunate brethren.[12] The separation of powers, between Zionist activity and messianic redemption, helped Rabbi Reines overcome two problems: it provided a response to criticism that saw Zionist activity as a violation of the halakhic prohibition against pushing back the end. Rabbi Reines' approach was also well integrated into the trend of Zionist coexistence between the Orthodox and the secular, a reality that necessitated significant concessions.

2 The Second Jubilee – From the Beginning of the 20th Century to the Establishment of the State of Israel

2.1 *Introduction*

With the development of the Zionist enterprise and the establishment of the new settlements, the question of the place of religion became more and more practical. The Second Aliyah (1904–1914) and the Third Aliyah (1918–1923) were different in their human composition from the First Aliyah. The members

12 For a different and more complex presentation of Reines' position, see, Dov Schwartz, *Religious Zionism as a Cultural Phenomenon –Introduction*, *in* Studies in Religious Zionism 9 (Yishai Arnon, Yehuda Friedlander & Dov Schwartz eds., 2012).

of the First Aliyah were mostly from observant families, but the immigrants in the next two Aliyahs were for the most part young people who abandoned the religious way of life. The pioneers who arrived in the colonies of the First Aliyah, brought with them a secular way of life, and they were joined by many decedents of the First Aliyah pioneers who dismantled the yoke of Torah and mitzvot and became secularized. The kibbutzim established by the second and third Aliyot pioneers had a distinctly secular character, and this character was also the case in the working-class neighborhoods that were established in the urban settlements. The Fourth Aliyah (1924–1931), consisted mainly of lower-middle-class families, joined the urban settlements that were developing, especially the city of Tel Aviv, which grew at a rapid pace. This immigration also included a large secular public.

In the reality of openly secular localities and other localities in which a large part of the population does not observe Torah and mitzvot, the discussion shifted to focus more and more on the nature of the public sphere. Naturally, the question of the proper nature of the public Sabbath was at the center of the discussion. Below we will describe two issues that preoccupied the Jewish public in Israel as well as the Zionist institutions in those years.

2.2 *The Struggle for the Character of the Sabbath in the Lands of the Nation*

As noted, the Second Aliyah brought with it large and organized groups of pioneers with a secular ideology and lifestyle. In the years 1909–1910, the first Kibbutzim were founded on the land of the Jewish National Fund, thus creating for the first time the reality of a non-observant community. Some of the new settlements were established near the old colonies, and thus the traditional residents of the colonies were exposed to the desecration of the Sabbath by the pioneers. In the summer of 1911, On the Shavuot holiday and the Shabbat adjacent to it, a large gathering of workers was held in the colony of Ein Ganim, near the village Petah Tikva, which involved the desecration of holidays and Shabbat. This organized event caused a deep shock among the religious public, and in its wake a protest meeting was convened in Jaffa in which Rabbi Kook, the rabbi of Jaffa at the time, spoke.[13]

Rabbi Kook appealed to the management of the JNF – the owner of the lands of the new groups and colonies – demanding that it enact an unequivocal provision prohibiting the desecration of Shabbat and Holiday on its lands.

---

13 For the text of his remarks, see, Avraham Wasserman & Eitam Henkin, To take root: Rabbi Abraham Isaac Kook and the Jewish National Fund 62–63 (2012) [hereinafter Wasserman & Henkin, To take root].

In addition, Rabbi Kook turned to the leaders of the Mizrachi and demanded that they raise a proposal at the Tenth Zionist Congress, which was about to convene about two months later, a resolution that would make obligatory the observance of the Sabbath and the festival in every settlement on the national land. The Mizrachi members did indeed raise a proposal in this spirit to the Congress, but the proposal met with opposition. In the end, it was decided not to issue a binding statement on this matter, but to make do with Herzl's declaration in the past that "Zionism will not do anything that will be against religion."[14]

About ten years later, at the 12th Zionist Congress held in 1921 in Carlsbad, Czechoslovakia, a resolution was passed, after a fierce debate, that "in the public actions of the institutions founded, maintained or supported by the Zionist Organization, nothing shall be done that harms Jewish tradition. The Executive of the Zionist Organization must ensure the implementation of this resolution." The resolution adopted general language, did not specify what the "offensive things" were, did not appoint those responsible for enforcing it on the ground, and did not include the imposition of sanctions on those who violated it. Therefore, it did not have the power to change the reality on the ground. At the next congress, held in 1923, the Mizrachi members complained about it, and in response Nahum Sokolov, the chairperson of the conference, said the following: "I emphasize that the resolution in this sense of the Twelfth Congress must take place, in order to ensure that every Jewish brother, even the most religious, has a free and joyful work in the great construction work."[15]

After the 13th Congress, Rabbi Kook called on the Congress not to be satisfied with declarations, but to "enact laws and fences" that would exclude any possibility of breaching the religious walls and desecrating the Sabbath on the nation's land. In the next five congresses, from the 14th to the 18th, the Mizrachi tried to pass a binding bill, in the spirit of Rabbi Kook's words. Specifically, they demanded that the contracts between the JNF management and the settlers be supplemented with a clause prohibiting the desecration of the Sabbath in public. Violation of which will result in fines and cancellation of the contract. The legislative attempts were repeatedly rebuffed by the delegates from the Secular Parties.

---

14 *Id.* at 64–67 and see more on this matter and its ramifications in Yehoshua Kaniel, Continuity and change 277–280 (1982).

15 Rivka Rinsky, Be'ayat ha-Shabbat ba-Yishuv ha-Yehudi be-Eretz Yisrael u-ve-Mosdot ha-Hanhagah ha-Tzionit ve-ha-Yishuvit bi-Shnot ha-Esrim ve-ha-Shloshim [The Problem of Shabbat in the Jewish Yishuv in Israel and in the Institutions of the Zionist and Yishuv Leadership in the 1920s and 1930s] 9 (1980) (M.A. thesis, Bar-Ilan University). [hereinafter Rinsky, The Problem of Shabbat].

In 1930, it was decided to add a clause to the lease contract with the JNF that obligates municipal tenants to observe the Sabbath on its properties.[16] The chairman of the Mizrachi party, Rabbi Meir Berlin, was not satisfied with this and demanded that a similar clause be included in the lease contract for agricultural land. Yossi Katz notes that the pressure to insert a clause on the observance of the Sabbath into the agricultural lease "did not come ... only on the part of ... Rabbi Berlin and other religious circles, but also from within the JNF itself. Indeed, its members saw the JNF as a popular body that appealed to all streams of Judaism, and they feared losing an entire sector of the donors and with it a significant share of the revenues."[17] The demand was supported by other members of the JNF's board of directors, among them Berl Katznelson, who was one of the leaders of Labor Zionism and was considered its moral and ideological compass. However, Berl and other members of the board of directors expressed great doubt about the effectiveness of the clause, that is, doubts about its ability to bring about a change in the current situation, especially if it did not include a public relations effort. Ultimately, at the end of 1933, After many years of pressure, a clause was inserted into the lease contract signed by the JNF with the settlers on the national lands, stating that "the lessee is obligated to strike on Shabbat and Jewish holidays from all kinds of work and crafts, from all field and vineyard work, and from industrial and commercial enterprises."[18]

In the same year, the Zionist General Council passed a resolution according to which it "views the return on the Sabbath from work and commerce not only as a matter of religious tradition, but also as a general national value, cultural and social, the observance of which applies to every Jew, regardless of his outlook on matters of religion and tradition."[19]

In August 1935, the 19th Zionist Congress convened. After the Mizrachi faction withdrew from all deliberations in the Congress, until a binding decision was made regarding the observance of the Sabbath on national lands, the following resolution was finally adopted: "The Congress approves the decision of the Zionist General Council regarding the obligation to observe the Sabbath

---

16 Yossi Katz, *Religion and Zionism in the Yishuv Era: The Sabbath Observance Clause in Lease Contracts between the Jewish National Fund and the Agricultural Settlements*, 78 Zion 207, 213 (2013) [hereinafter Katz, *Religion and Zionism*].

17 *Id.* at 216.

18 Wasserman & Henkin, To take root, *supra* note 13, at 128–129.

19 Yisrael Kolat, *Dat Hevra u-Medina bi-Tkufat ha-Bayit ha-Leumi* [*Religion, Society and State in the Period of the National Home*], in Zionism and Religion 329, 360 (Shmuel Almog, Yehuda Reinharz & Anita Shapira eds., 1994); Katz, *Religion and Zionism*, *supra* note 16, at 224.

and Jewish holidays, and to take a sabbatical from work in construction and in the fields, in the vineyard, in industry and commerce. The Congress instructs the Executive to ensure that the resolution is upheld by all the legal means included in the Regulations of the Zionist Organization."[20]

Despite the inclusion of the Sabbath observance clause in the lease contract and the provision regarding its enforcement, the institutions of the Zionist movement did not act to implement the decision. The religious elements exerted pressure in this direction, and finally, in March 1937, a decision was made that determined, inter alia, that "a settlement or settler who does not stop the problem of desecrating the Sabbath, the JNF will sue him before a single arbitrator, in accordance with the clause stipulated in the contract."[21] This decision also did not lead to any real change on the ground, and in practice there were a few attempts to invoke the arbitration clause against Shabbat violators (and they too only against tenants of properties in the urban settlement, and not in the working settlement). In this reality, a pattern of protest letters sent to the JNF by religious elements became more and more established, "alongside public information activities and attempts made by the JNF to persuade settlers to observe the Sabbath, in a pleasant and untimely manner, and sometimes by way of 'empty threats' of punitive measures."[22] The Sabbath observance clause that the representatives of the religious fought for has in fact become a dead letter.

2.3 *The Shabbat Struggles in Tel Aviv*

Parallel to the struggle that took place in the Zionist institutions, an arena of struggle also developed in the first Hebrew city, Tel Aviv. In 1922–1923, negotiations were held between Tel Aviv and several Jewish neighborhoods in Jaffa, which had a traditional and religious character, to join the city of Tel Aviv. As part of the negotiations, the residents of the neighborhoods demanded, as a condition for their joining, that Tel Aviv Municipality will enact a bylaw that will require the observance of the Sabbath in the municipal public area. After a long debate, it was agreed not to agree, meaning that the question of observing the Sabbath in the city of Tel Aviv would be brought to the future council of the united city for discussion and would not be a stumbling block for the unification.[23]

20 *see* Katz, *Religion and Zionism id.*

21 *Id* at 227.

22 *Id* at 231.

23 Ilan Shchouri, Chalom She'hafach Le'khrakh: Tel Aviv, Leidah u-Tzmicha – Ha'ir She'holida Medinah [A Dream That Became a Metropolis: Tel Aviv, Birth and Growth – The City That Gave Birth to a State] 207 (new ed. 2013).

After the unification, the residents of the neighborhoods and representatives of the religious public in Tel Aviv continued to demand the enactment of a binding law. At the end of 1925, a bylaw was passed as follows: "Any store except a restaurant and any factory shall not open on the Jewish Sabbath within the territory of the Tel Aviv local council, the prohibition shall not apply to a Christian and Muslim store or factory."[24]

In 1928, a Jewish café owner named Altshuler was convicted of violating the bylaw and fined 2 pounds. The Supreme Court, which consisted of two British judges and one Jewish judge, invalidated the bylaw by a majority opinion.[25] The Tel Aviv Municipality saw the repeal of the law as a violation of the Jewish public's right to civil autonomy within its cities and towns, which gave the issue a national dimension. The transformation of the issue into a national matter has led to the fact that even a public for which the Sabbath has not been at the forefront of its priorities has now joined the struggle. The Tel Aviv Municipality also shared the issue with the national institutions – the National Agency, the Chief Rabbinate and the Zionist Administration – and began a series of legal consultations in an attempt to enact a new bylaw that would ensure the creation of a public Sabbath observance and overcome the legal hurdle. These efforts were opposed by the British Mandate authorities. After a long struggle that lasted several years, in 1937 a bylaw was passed for Tel Aviv, which stated as follows: "Most businesses will remain closed on Saturdays and holidays. Eateries and cafes will only be able to serve meals indoors, until 10 p.m. on Saturday and holiday eves, and from 10 a.m. to 3 p.m. on Saturdays and holidays. The offenders will be fined a maximum of 10 Israeli pounds."[26]

The municipality began trying to enforce the new law but then met with stubborn opposition from some business owners. The municipality understood that if it used its power against the cafes that are open on the Sabbath, it could get into a tangle of lawsuits that would harm its sovereignty vis-à-vis the British government, and therefore it was careful not to impose sanctions against those who broke the law. Anat Hellman sums up the situation as follows: "The debate over the image of the Tel Aviv Sabbath remained unresolved.

24 Rinsky, The Problem of Shabbat, *supra* note 15, at 28.

25 MA 18/28 Attorney General v. Altshuler, 1 PLR 283, 286 (1928) (Palestine). For more information, see, Gideon Sapir, *"Bayamim ha-Hem ba-Zman ha-Zeh"?: – Al ha-Domeh ve-al ha-Shoneh Bein Shnei Ma'avakim be-Inyan Chakikat Shabbat be-Tel Aviv* [*"In Those Days at This Time"? – On the similarities and differences between two struggles regarding Shabbat legislation in Tel Aviv*], 34 Bar-ilan Law Studies (forthcoming 2025).

26 Quoted in the article by Anat Hellman, *Torah, Avodah u-Vatei Kafeh: Dat u-Farhesya be-Tel-Aviv ha-Mandatorit* [*Religion and the Public Sphere in Mandatory Tel Aviv*] 105 Kathedra 85, 105 (2002).

The Tel Aviv Municipality, which tried to reconcile between the parties, was exposed in all its weakness and was forced to skip both counts."[27]

The "Sabbath Law" in Tel Aviv was only partially enforced and did not revolutionize the life of the city, but the legislation in Tel Aviv had an impact outside the city. Many local authorities followed in Tel Aviv's footsteps and enacted bylaws on the subject of the Sabbath, the wording of which was based on the version adopted in Tel Aviv. Until the establishment of the State of Israel, bylaws for the observance of the Sabbath were enacted in seventeen Jewish localities. In these localities, the culture of recreation was less developed than in Tel Aviv, and the laws were enforced more effectively. It can therefore be said that the "Sabbath Law" of Tel Aviv laid the basis for an arrangement in the field of Shabbat that was anchored after the establishment of the State of Israel in the Status Quo arrangement, the circumstances of which will be discussed in the next chapter.

---

27 *Id.* at 110.

CHAPTER 2

From the Establishment of the State until the Electoral Upset

1 How Was the Status Quo Born and What Was Its Content?

For years, the accepted answer to the question, "How are matters of religion and state regulated in Israel?" was: "Through the status quo arrangement."[1] Status quo is a term derived from the expression 'status quo ante bellum', which means in Latin 'the situation that existed before the war'. In our context, this means that the arrangements in the area of religion-state relations enjoy long-term stability.

When was the status quo born? What led to its formation? What was its content? What contributed to its survival over a long period of time?

The first two questions were given several answers. According to one explanation, which for years was considered consensual by scholars of the period, the status quo was born in 1947. After Britain announced the return of the mandate to administer the territory it had received from the United Nations, the United Nations appointed a committee to advise on what to do with the territory that Britain was about to vacate. The members of the committee were about to visit Israel, and the leadership of the Jewish Agency sought to ensure that all the elements in the Jewish community presented a united front to the committee and supported the establishment of a Jewish state. Against this background, negotiations were held with members of the ultra-orthodox Agudat Yisrael movement, the results of which were summarized in a letter sent by the Agency's management to the heads of Agudat Yisrael.

> *Shabbat* – "It is clear that the legal day of rest in the Jewish state will be the Sabbath, and members of other religions will be able to rest on their weekly holiday."

---

1 See, for example, Michael Corinaldi, *Chofesh ha-Dat be-Yisrael – Bamah Nishtanah ha-Status Quo* [*Freedom of Religion in Israel – How the 'Status Quo' Has Changed*], 3 Sha'arei Mishpat 287, 290 (2003); Shuki Friedman, The Erosion of the Status Quo in the Religions between Religion and State in Israel 11 (Isr. Democracy Inst., Policy Paper No. 126, 2019) [hereinafter Friedman, The Erosion] ; Gal Levy, *Ve-Gam Elu Hen Toldot ha-Status Quo: Dat, Ma'amad ve-Etniyut be-Yisrael* [*And Too These Are the History of the Status Quo: Religion, Class, and Ethnicity in Israel*], 55 Megamot 275, 284 (2020).

 | DOI:10.1163/9789004758889_004

> *Kosher* – "We must take all the necessary measures to ensure that every state kitchen aimed at Jews has kosher food."
> *Marital law* – "everything possible will be done in order to accommodate in this matter the deep aspiration of the religious community, to prevent, G-d forbid, the division of the House of Israel into two."
> *Education* – "full autonomy of each stream of education will be guaranteed, and the State will set the 'minimum of compulsory education' in subjects such as Hebrew, history and science."

According to this explanation, the status quo arrangement was born as a result of arm-twisting on the part of Agudat Yisrael, which took advantage of the Zionist movement's distress on the eve of the establishment of the state. It is not surprising, then, that there were those who adopted this explanation and used it to attack the ultra-orthodox public.[2] Sociologist Menachem Friedman disagrees with this explanation.[3] He points out that at the time the letter was sent, no one regarded it as a commitment to maintain the status quo in religious matters in the State of Israel. Moreover, an examination of the "commitments" contained in the letter shows that their content was far from allaying the concerns of the ultra-orthodox public, and in this sense, the letter could not fulfill the role attributed to it. For example, at the beginning of the letter it was emphasized that the establishment of the state was conditional on the approval of the United Nations, and its approval is conditional on ensuring equal rights and full freedom of conscience for all citizens – a condition that is inconsistent with a commitment to base personal status arrangements on Torah law, as demanded by the Agudat Yisrael. Similarly, there is no commitment to keep kosher in public kitchens.

If Friedman is right, and the status quo was not formed on the eve of the establishment of the state, when was it born? Some believe that it was born later. In their opinion, the general principle of maintaining the status quo was born in the negotiations between Mapai and the United Religious Front, after the elections for the Constituent Assembly, while the detailed arrangements included in it were formulated over the following years.[4]

2 See, for example, Shulamit Aloni, Ha-Hesder: Mi-Medinat Chok le-Medinat Halacha [The Arrangement: From a State of Law to a State of Halacha] (1970).

3 Menachem Friedman, *The chronicle of the Status Quo: Religion and State in Israel, in* Transition from "Yishuv" to State 1947–1949: Continuity and Change 47, 47–65 (Varda Pilowsky ed., 1988).

4 See, for example, Yoel Raffel, Yachasei Datiyim-Chiloniyim ba-Shanah ha-Rishonah la-Medinah [Religious-Secular Relations in the First Year of the State], in Shanah Rishonah

What, according to this view, led to the agreement? There are two explanations for this. According to one explanation, the agreement was reached due to coalition calculations.[5] In the elections for the Constituent Assembly, held in January 1949, the Workers Party in the Land of Israel (Mapai), headed by David Ben-Gurion, won. Mapai did not win an absolute majority, and needed a partnership in order to form a government. Ostensibly, its natural partner was supposed to be the United Workers Party (Mapam), a sister party, whose views were close to those of Mapai. However, two reasons caused Ben-Gurion to refrain from relying on Mapam: There was concern that this would help strengthen Mapam, which at the time was a real competitor for the primacy, and a lack of clarity regarding Mapam's ideological loyalty, which, along with its commitment to the State of Israel, maintained a strong connection to the Soviet Union. Under these circumstances, the religious parties that ran in a joint list were relatively comfortable partners. Nor did they threaten Mapai's hegemony, nor were their positions on many issues far from Mapai's. In the socio-economic sphere, no special adjustments were required, since both among the ultra-orthodox and among the religious Zionists, the social-democratic idea enjoyed dominance (Poalei Agudat Yisrael and Hapoel Mizrachi, respectively). In matters of foreign affairs and security, the religious public was not characterized as hawkish at the time. The only area in which it was necessary to bridge the gaps in perspective was religion, and under these circumstances, after negotiations, a compromise was reached that satisfied both sides.

According to a second explanation, Ben-Gurion's choice to reach a compromise on matters of religion and state did not stem from coalition constraints, but was based on a conscious decision in favor of adopting a consociational solution.[6] Consociational Democracy is described by political scientists as a way of running a state in which there are deep social rifts: the elites representing the various sides agree that each side will have a share in the leadership of the state and the institutions of government, and that each side will have the right of veto, and the possibility of managing certain affairs autonomously. According to this explanation, Ben-Gurion did not really "need" the religious

le-Atzma'ut 1948–1949 [The First Year of Independence 1948–1949] 127, 141 (Mordechai Naor ed., 1988).

5 See, for example, Daniel Friedman, Before the Revolution – Law and Politics in the Age of Innocence 170 (2015).

6 See, for example, Eliezer Don-Yahiya, The Politics of accommodation: settling conflicts or state and Religious in Israel (1997); Asher Cohen & Baruch Zisser, *Mi-Demokratia Hesderit le-Demokratia Mashberit: ha-Ma'avak al ha-Zehut ha-Kolektivit be-Yisrael* [*From Arrangement Democracy to Crisis Democracy: The Struggle for Collective Identity in Israel*], 3 POLITIKA 9 (1999).

parties. The concessions he made did not stem from the need to include them in the coalition. On the contrary, Ben-Gurion chose to include the religious parties in power in order to bridge the rifts and strengthen social cohesion among the people living in Zion.

Ron Haris disagrees with the previous two explanations, at least partially. He argues that some of the arrangements in the realm of religion and state were not created intentionally but were born as a result of omission.[7] In order to understand his argument, we must expand a bit on the situation that prevailed on the eve of the establishment of the state. After the United Nations decided to adopt the Partition Plan, Ben-Gurion appointed a number of committees, whose role was to prepare what was required for the establishment of the state in various fields. Ben-Gurion entrusted the legal field with Dov Yosef, who established a "legal council" tasked with drafting the laws of the state in the making. The council failed to fulfill its role. Several factors contributed to this, including the fact that Ben-Gurion attached relatively little importance to the legal field and therefore did not devote much effort to its success, and the security situation that prevailed in the country at the time, which prevented the possibility of regular gatherings and orderly discussions.

After the establishment of the State of Israel, and in the absence of a suitable alternative, the Provisional State Council – the body to which the Declaration of Independence assigned the role of the provisional legislature until the establishment of a permanent legislature – enacted the Law and Government Ordinance (Paxashoum). Section 11 of the Paxashoom stipulates that the law that was practiced in the Land of Israel on the eve of the establishment of the State will remain in force. On the eve of the establishment of the State of Israel, the religious sought to grant a special status to Jewish law, but Article 11 adopted the rule that had prevailed until then, which granted a special status to English common law. Section 17 of the Pakshom stipulated that the existing courts would continue to function. On the eve of the establishment of the State, there were those who sought to abolish the religious monopoly in the field of personal status – which was practiced during the British Mandate period, and maintained the status quo that existed during the Ottoman period – but Article 17 fixed the existing situation.

7 Ron Haris, *Hizdamnuyot Historiot ve-Hachmatzot be-Hesach ha-Da'at – Al Shiluvo shel ha-Mishpat ha-Ivri ba-Mishpat ha-Yisraeli be-Et Hakamat ha-Medinah* [*Historical Opportunities and Missed Opportunities: On the Integration of Jewish Law into Israeli Law at the Establishment of the State of Israel*], *in* Shnei Evrei ha-Gesher: Dat u-Medinah be-Reshit Darka shel Yisrael [On Both Sides of the Bridge: Religion and State in Israel's Early Journey] 21 (Mordechai Bar-On and Zvi Tzameret eds., 2002).

What were the contents of the status quo?

The status quo has never been defined in detail. However, it was customary to include, at a minimum, the following areas:

Education – In 1953, the State Education Law was enacted. As part of the law, the education system was divided into three tracks, two official, state and state-religious, and one recognized non-official – independent ultra-orthodox education.

Military service – During the War of Independence, a group of yeshiva students received an exemption from the obligation to enlist in the IDF. Over the years, an arrangement was established in which the Minister of Defense granted a postponement of the obligation to enlist yeshiva students. In most cases, the postponement became a complete exemption.

Conditions of service in the army – The IDF enshrined in its orders the obligation to maintain the kosher of kitchens and food, to strike from routine activities during the Sabbath, and to allow the religious soldier to observe the commandments of religion.

Kashrut – The Chief Rabbinate was granted exclusivity over the granting of kosher certificates, and kashrut was maintained in the official kitchens.

Religious Services – The status and budget of the religious councils responsible for providing various religious services is enshrined in the law.[8]

Shabbat – In 1951, the Hours of Work and Rest Law was passed, which established the Sabbath as the official day of rest, and prohibited the employment of Jewish workers on the Sabbath, unless a permit was granted. In 1969, the prohibition on working on the Sabbath was expanded, to include employers and independent workers. The decision regarding the opening of businesses on the Sabbath was delegated to the local level, and many local authorities enacted bylaws that imposed restrictions on the opening of businesses on the Sabbath. The granting of a license to operate public transportation lines on the Sabbath was conditional on the cessation of its activity on the Sabbath. With the exception of the Haifa area (and later Eilat as well), where public transportation operated on Saturdays as well.

8 The religious councils were established during the Mandate period, and their status was regulated by law even before the establishment of the state. See Religious Communities (Organization) Ordinance, 1926, HEI 70 1292 (Palestine).

Personal status – It was determined that marriage and divorce would be conducted in Israel according to religious law. At least in the beginning, religious law was also given dominance in all matters relating to financial questions involved in divorce. The religious courts were given exclusivity over the issue of divorce and a parallel status to the civil courts in all matters related to financial matters involving divorce. Regarding Jews, section 2 of the Rabbinical Courts Jurisdiction (Marriage and Divorce) Law, enacted in 1953, states that "the marriage and divorce of Jews shall be conducted in Israel in accordance with Torah law." Section 1 of the law states that "matters of marriage and divorce of Jews in Israel who are citizens or residents of the State shall be under the exclusive jurisdiction of the rabbinical courts."

For many years, the status quo maintained impressive stability. Evidence of this stability can be found in the coalition agreements signed between the ruling Mapai party and the National Religious Party.[9] Contributing to this stability was the "historic alliance," as it was commonly called, which strengthened the relationship of trust between Mapai, and its successor, the Labor Party, and the National Religious Party.

The fact that the status quo generally enjoys stability does not mean that matters of religion and state have not been at the center of political crises from time to time. Suffice it to mention the crisis over the question of education in the immigrant camps,[10] or the dispute over who is a Jew for the purposes of the Law of Return and the Population Registry Law,[11] two issues on which the struggles threatened the integrity of the coalition. The issue of the Sabbath was also not absent from the agenda of the political system.[12] Moreover, despite the declaration of a freeze on the status quo, over the years there have been certain changes in the arrangements in the realm of religion and state, in theory or in

9 See, for example, 69 DK 706 (1974) (Coalition Agreement between the Alignment, the National Religious Party, and the Independent Liberal Party); 56 DK 271 (1970) (Coalition Agreement between the Israeli Labor Party, Gush Herut-Liberals (Gahal), the National Religious Party, and the Independent Liberal Party).

10 For more information, see, Zvi Tzameret, *The Frumkin Commission – The Investigation of Allegations Concerning the Education of New Immigrant*, 1 Iyunim Bitkumat Israel 405 (1999).

11 For more information, see, Shahar Lifshitz & Gideon Sapir, *Who Shall Decides Who is a Jew – On the Proper Role of the Judiciary in a Democratic Society*, 22 Bar-ilan Law Studies 269 (2006).

12 For further information, see, *Gideon Sapir, "And You Called Shabbat a Delight?"? Work Trade and Leisure in the Sabbath in Israel – 1948–2017* ,31 Bar-ilan Law Studies 583 (2018).

practice. However, these deviations do not contradict the assertion that during these decades the status quo has been maintained in general.

2 The Court's Attitude to the Status Quo

The stability of the status quo in the first three decades of the state's existence was also facilitated by the fact that the agreements reached in the political system were not usually challenged by the courts. From the very beginning of its establishment, the Supreme Court did not shy away from confronting the political system in cases where it believed that it unjustifiably violated individual rights.[13] However, in the first decades of its existence, the Court tried to maintain a distinction between legal questions, which it agreed to deal with, and questions involving ideological dispute, which it tried to avoid.

One of the tools by which the court was able to avoid dealing with the moral disputes that were placed before it were the doctrines of standing and justiciability, two grounds whose use enabled the court to dismiss petitions out of hand, without considering them on their merits.[14]

For example, in 1970, Israel Becker, a reserve officer, filed a petition with the Supreme Court against the policy in which the Minister of Defense granted a postponement and exemption from military service to yeshiva students. The court rejected the petition out of hand after ruling that the petitioner had not proven that the said policy harmed him in a unique way, and therefore he did not comply with the threshold requirement for the right of standing.[15]

Although in general the court's conduct was characterized by restraint with regard to disputes of values in general and in particular in matters of religion and state, from time to time the court chose to deal with these matters as well, and in most cases it tipped the scales in favor of the "secular" position. For example, at the end of the 1960s, the Broadcasting Authority, which until then had broadcast only on the radio, began broadcasting on television as well. The Authority also sought to broadcast on the Sabbath, but the religious objected to this. This sparked controversy and petitions were filed with the court on both sides of the fence. The court rejected a petition against the broadcasts on Shabbat, on the grounds that the petitioner lacked standing,[16] but accepted

---

13 See, for example, HCJ 73/53 Kol Ha'am Co. v. Minister of the Interior, 7 PD 873 (1953).

14 For more information, see, 4 Daphne Barak-Erez, Administrative Law – Procedural Administrative Law Ch. 36 – (2017) [hereinafter: Barak-Erez, Administrative Law].

15 HCJ 40/70 Becker v. Minister of Defense, 24(1) PD. 238 (1970).

16 HCJ 287/69 Meron v. Minister of Labor, 24(1) PD 337 (1970).

a petition against a temporary decision made by the government to suspend the start of broadcasts on Shabbat until after a government discussion on the matter is held.[17] The court's rulings have led to the fact that the television channels operate on the Sabbath as well. However, even in cases where it chose to intervene, the court usually used formal and technical reasons and refrained from basing its decision on moral reasons.[18] The minor tone used by the court even in cases where it chose to intervene somewhat reduced the intensity of the religious criticism of the decisions made.

An exception to the court's refusal to intervene in the content of the status quo related to a number of issues that, in the opinion of many, have violated the basic rights of citizens. The most prominent example of this is the area of personal status, in which religious law and the religious establishment have been given precedence. Formally, the possibility of civil marriage does not exist in Israel, but in a precedent-setting ruling given in the 1960s, the Supreme Court opened the door for the recognition of this marriage.[19] Ms. Funk, a Christian Israeli resident, and Mr. Schlesinger, a Jewish citizen, were married in Cyprus in a civil marriage. Upon their return to Israel, the couple applied to the Ministry of Interior to be registered in the Population Registry as married. The Ministry of Interior rejected the request on the grounds that the possibility of civil marriage was not available to Israeli citizens. The couple petitioned the High Court of Justice and their petition was accepted. The main reason given by the court for its decision was that the registration of personal status was intended for statistical purposes only and lacks any evidentiary validity. Therefore, the registration of the Funk-Schlesingers as married does not constitute recognition by the state of the validity of their marriage, and therefore there is no impediment to granting the request and registering them as married.

Ostensibly, the court's decision in the Funk-Schlesinger case was of no practical significance because it dealt only with registration for statistical purposes, but in fact it was a decision that led to a revolution in the legal regulation of marriage in Israel. In practice, the government authorities examine the marital status of the couple according to the registry, and do not look for independent evidence to support the representation that emerges from the registry. This is also the case with the rights of married couples vis-à-vis individuals or private entities. Practically, couples married in a civil marriage today enjoy

---

17 HCJ 281/69 Prime Minister of Israel v. Kaplan and the Broadcasting Authority, 23(2) PD 394 (1969).

18 For further details, see, Menachem Mautner, *The Decline of Formalism and the Rise of Values, in* Law & The Culture of Israel 90–98 (2011).

19 HCJ 143/62 Schlesinger v. Minister of the Interior, 17 PD 225 (1963).

all the rights of couples married in a religious service. Therefore, contrary to the argument of the majority justices in the Funk-Schlesinger case, the registry has great practical significance, and not only symbolic.[20] In this ruling, the Supreme Court legalized civil marriages conducted abroad for Israeli citizens. This move also allowed citizens of the country to circumvent religious law on the question of eligibility to marry. If the registration of the status in the population registry has no evidentiary validity, it is also possible to register as married couples who, according to Halacha, cannot marry.

For many years, the court has repeatedly said that the order to register as married Israeli spouses who were married in a civil marriage abroad does not reflect recognition of the validity of this marriage. But in 2003, the court took another step, and in a revolutionary judgment – the interesting background of which cannot be laid out here – recognized the full validity of civil marriages that took place abroad.[21] The court further ruled that since the halakha did not regulate the question of financial relations between couples married in a civil marriage, the unique jurisdiction in these matters is vested in the civil court, and the rabbinical court does not have parallel jurisdiction in these matters. The result of this ruling is that alongside the option of religious marriage, which is enshrined in the Rabbinical Courts Jurisdiction Law, there is also option for civil marriages (conducted abroad) in Israel.

Another way in which the court has reduced the religious monopoly in marital matters is through the institution of common-law couples, i.e. couples who live together, share a household, and sometimes have children, all without being officially married – some because they could not be officially married in Israel, and some because they chose to avoid marriage. The Supreme Court included these couples in the legal definition of "common-law couples," and almost completely aligned their status to that of married couples. Other countries also recognize the status of common-law couples, but in Israel, the recognition is particularly broad and deep.[22] Jewish couples in Israel who choose the common-law route do not marry, and therefore sections 1–2 of the Rabbinical Courts Jurisdiction Law do not apply to them at all. This means that the Rabbinical Court has no jurisdiction to hear their case, and religious law is irrelevant to them.[23]

---

20 See, Eitan Levontin, *A Tower Floating in the Air: Funk-Schlesinger and the Law of the Population Registry*, 11 Mishpat Umishmal 129 (2007).

21 HCJ 8638/03 Amir v. The Great Rabbinical Court of Jerusalem, 61(1) PD 259 (2006).

22 See, Shahar Lifshitz, Cohabitation Law in Israel in Light of Civil Law Theory of the Family (2005).

23 In 2010, another path of creating a relationship was born, which allows couples who are not part of the recognized religious communities in Israel to enter into a spousal

Elsewhere, I argued that despite the gradual weakening of the religious monopoly on marriage and divorce in Israel, it is still troubling from the perspective of the liberal outlook. The right to marry is recognized worldwide, and the State of Israel does not meet all the conditions for its realization. The alternatives of civil marriage abroad and of a common-law couple institution do not fully reconcile the tension between this monopoly and the right to marry, even though they weaken it.[24] Yet, although this practical solution is not sufficient, its gradual formation, through the court's rulings, has somewhat reduced the pressing need for reform in this area.

covenant – "an agreement between spouses to live together and maintain a family life and a joint household" – and to register in the Couple's Partnership Registry. See, Civil Union Law for the Religionless, 5770–2010, SH 2235 428, https://www.nevo.co.il/law_html/law00/73488.htm.

24 See, Daniel Statman & Gideon Sapir, State and Religion in Israel – A Philosophical-Legal Inquiry ch. 9 (2019).

CHAPTER 3

From the Electoral Upset to the End of the 20th Century

The last two decades of the 20th century have been characterized by two phenomena. The first is the gradual collapse of the status quo, and the second is the awakening of the public discourse on questions of religion and state. We will describe the two developments,[1] and offer a number of explanations for each.

1 The Collapse of the Status Quo

One of the main factors in the (relative) stability of the status quo during the first three decades of the state's existence was the (also relative) stability of the political system. In each of the first eight elections, the formation of the government was assigned to the leader of Mapai, and in all cases Mapai chose the National Religious Party as a partner. The judicial restraint adopted by the Supreme Court also contributed to stability: The Court generally refrained from intervening in disputes over questions of values, including matters of religion and state. Over the next two decades, the reality on these two issues changed drastically, and this significantly undermined the stability of the status quo.[2]

1.1 *Changes in the Political Map*

The festive election broadcast on Israeli television, which began immediately after the polling stations closed in the elections for the Ninth Knesset, in 1977, began with the words of the legendary television presenter, Haim Yavin: "Ladies and gentlemen, an Electoral Upset!" Likud leader Menachem Begin, who had spent many years in the political desert, hurried to the Western Wall Plaza to thank the Creator for the victory.

---

1 For a detailed description of the collapse of the status quo on several key issues, see Friedman, The Erosion, *supra* note 28, at 37.

2 For further information, see Asher Cohen & Baruch Zisser, Mehashlama Lehaslama: ha-Shesa ha-Dati-Hiloni be-Fetach ha-Me'ah ha-Esrim ve-Achat [From Acceptance to Escalation: The Religious-Secular Rift at the Beginning of the Twenty-First Century] (2003) [hereinafter Cohen & Zisser, Mehashlama Lehaslama].

 | DOI:10.1163/9789004758889_005

The Likud's rise to power had a significant impact on the stability of the status quo. Two factors contributed to this: First, on matters of religion and state, the Likud's approach was more sympathetic to the religious position than that of the Labor Party, the successor to Mapai, and this encouraged the religious parties that joined the coalition to present new demands in the field of religion and state. Second, the hegemony that the left had lost did not shift permanently to the right. Over the next two decades, the Labor Party and the Likud competed, without one of them gaining clear dominance. The competition between the two major parties strengthened the bargaining power of the religious parties. This assertion should be somewhat qualified. During this period, a unity government was served twice with the participation of the two major parties,[3] a reality in which the religious parties became to some extent a fifth wheel in the wagon, which actually weakened their bargaining power. Either way, in the new reality, old alliances were forgotten, restraint was abandoned, and the political market was opened to lively bargaining activity.

The change in the rules of the game gave birth, among other things, to a series of laws of a religious nature that were passed by the Knesset in the first years after the revolution. These include the Foundations of Law Act, 1980, which (ostensibly) granted Jewish law status as a source of filling gaps in the law; the Chief Rabbinate Act of that year, which gathered under one roof the powers and method of election of the Chief Rabbis and the Chief Rabbinate Council; the Prohibition of Fraud in Kashrut Act of 1983, which assigns the authority to grant a kosher certificate to the Chief Rabbinate and to rabbis authorized by it for this purpose; and the Matzot (Chametz Prohibitions) Act of 1986, which states that during Passover, "a business owner shall not publicly display a chametz product for sale or consumption."

The practical impact of these laws in matters of religion and state in Israel was minimal, either because they did not really innovate anything (like the Chief Rabbinate Law) or because later on the court gave them an interpretation that emptied them of any real content.[4] At the same time, however, a number of decisions were made in the political system, which, although not

3 These are the two unity governments that served after the elections for the 12th Knesset (1984–1988) and the 13th Knesset (1988–1992).

4 This is especially true in relation to The Foundations of Law Act and the Matzot Holiday Law. For more information, see, Benjamin Porat, A Proposal to Amend the Foundations of Law Act, with an Analysis and Critique (2016); CrimC (MC Jerusalem) 4726/07 State of Israel v. Terminal Twenty One Ltd., Nevo Legal Database (Apr. 2, 2008); Ayala Goldberg & Ariel Finkelstein, Skira: Isur Hatzagat Chametz Kim'at she-Eino Ne'echaf be-Rov ha-Aretz [Review: The Prohibition on Displaying Chametz is Almost Not Enforced in Most of the Country] (Isr. Democracy Inst., 2023), https://www.idi.org.il/articles/48914.

enshrined in primary legislation, had a significant impact on the situation in this area. A major change occurred in the issue of the enlistment of yeshiva students. Until 1977, two restrictions were imposed on the arrangement of postponement of enlistment. First, quotas were set for the number of yeshiva students who could postpone their enlistment. Second, only young people who had studied in high school in yeshiva educational institutions could join the arrangement. The first restriction was lifted by the first Begin government in 1977, and in 1981, the second restriction was removed. These two changes contributed to a significant increase in the number of young people receiving exemptions or postponements from military service each year, a volume that has been increasing, due to the natural growth among the ultra-orthodox sector.

Another important change occurred, during this period, in the scope of the government's support, both direct and indirect, to the ultra-orthodox sector.[5] The growing influence of the sector in the field of budgeting was contributed by the fact that immediately after Electoral Upset, the chairmanship of the Knesset Finance Committee was given to the Agudat Yisrael party, and the position remained in its hands in the next two Knessets as well.

1.2 *The Change in the Court's Policy*

The de facto nullification of the threshold grounds:

The High Court of Justice has broad discretion in deciding whether to allow the petitioner to present his argument before the court. Over the years, the Court has developed a series of "threshold grounds," that the petitioner must overcome for his case to be heard. Two of the grounds: "standing" and "justiciability" have often been used by the first generation of judges of the court as a means of avoiding dealing with issues that they think should not have been dealt with. With the appointment of Aharon Barak to the Supreme Court in the late 1970s, the erosion of the threshold grounds began, until towards the end of the 1980s, these two grounds were almost completely abolished.[6] This move enabled the court to expand its jurisdiction and intervene in issues that the High Court of Justice had previously refrained from addressing, including disputes over matters of religion and state.

---

5 See, for example, Shahar Ilan, Haredim Ltd 185–202 (2000); On the other hand, see, Hadar Lipshits, *Budgeting for Ultra-orthodox Education – The Failure of Ultra-orthodox Politics 1996–2006*, 135 Israel Studies 20 (2015), which points to the fact that between 1996 and 2006, the state's budget for ultra-orthodox education, per student, decreased in comparison to the budget, per student, in State schools.

6 See, Barak-Erez, Administrative Law, *supra* note 41.

Since the beginning of the 1970s, various petitioners have tried to attack the arrangement in which yeshiva students are deferred from the obligation to enlist in the IDF, a defferal that ultimately turns into a full exemption from the obligation to serve in the army. As stated, the first petition was filed in 1970.[7] The petitioner presented himself as having a personal interest in the matter, since he is "a student by profession and a reserve officer with the rank of lieutenant". The court rejected the petition on the grounds of lack of justiciability and lack of standing.

The next petition was filed in 1981, and it was also dismissed outright.[8] However, a petition filed in the mid-1980s, marks a turning point in the court's approach to the issue.[9] Although the court rejected the petition, this time it did so after hearing it, and did not reject it outright. The rejection of the petition was based on the determination that the scope of the exemption for yeshiva students does not reach dimensions that require a determination of unreasonableness.

This ruling carried with it the seeds of change that indeed took place in a judgment, at the end of the 1990s.[10] The court then came out, for the first time, against the exemption arrangement, and ruled that it was illegal. The court ruled that the Minister of Defense was not given the authority to exempt all yeshiva students, but only to grant an individual exemption. This argument was based on the interpretive presumption that such arrangements ("primary arrangements") should be determined by the legislature, and therefore it is unlikely that the legislature intended to delegate to the Minister of Defense the authority to decide on granting sweeping exemption to all yeshiva students. The court returned the question to the legislature without explicitly determining whether a decision by the Knesset to anchor the same arrangement in primary legislation will pass constitutional review.

The High Court's violation of the status quo was expressed not only in the change or cancellation of arrangements in the field of religion-state relations, but also in the weakening of religious institutions. Thus, for example, the High Court of Justice subordinated the rabbinical courts to its authority on the substantive level,[11] and deprived them of the authority to hear certain matters,

---

7 HCJ 40/70 Becker v. Minister of Defense, 24(1) PD 238, 246 (1970).

8 HCJ 448/81 Ressler v. Minister of Defense, 36(1) PD 81 (1981). A request for a further hearing of this judgment was rejected by the President of the Supreme Court, Moshe Landau. LCivA2/82 Ressler v. Minister of Defense, 37(1) PD 708 (1982).

9 HCJ 910/86 Ressler v. Minister of Defense, 42(2) PD 441 (1988).

10 HCJ 3267/97 Rubinstein v. Minister of Defense, 49(5) PD 481 (1998).

11 See, HCJ 1000/92 Bavli v. The Great Rabbinical Court, 48(2) PD 221 (1994). In this judgment, it was determined that apart from issues related to marriage and divorce, the

even though the rabbinical court had dealt with these matters for a long time.[12] The High Court also intervened in the discretion of the Chief Rabbinate in various fields,[13] as well as in the activity, composition and manner of election of the religious councils.[14] These moves have been a source of frustration for some of the Religious Zionist public, which attaches importance to the existence and official status of these institutions. The ultra-orthodox do not attach the same importance to these state religious institutions, but nevertheless, they too resented what they perceived as blatant and illegitimate interference in arrangements on matters of religion and state that were accepted by consensus in the political system.

1.2.1 The Constitutional Revolution

From the establishment of the State of Israel until 1995, the State of Israel did not have a formal human rights bill.[15] Although the Declaration of Independence promised a constitution, a public debate that lasted almost two years made it clear that the adoption of a constitution was still not possible. The effort to enact a constitution encountered many stumbling blocks, including the failure to bridge deep differences of values and the reluctance of the ruling Mapai party, headed by David Ben-Gurion, to adopt a constitution that would limit the power of the government. After it became clear that it was impossible to enact a constitution, the Knesset accepted in 1950 a compromise proposal: The process of establishing the constitution would be carried out in stages, in the form of basic laws that would be consolidated when the process was completed.

---

rabbinical court must rule in accordance with civil legal norms. Thus, it was deprived of its authority to adjudicate according to halakhic rules in matters of property involving a divorce claim filed in the court.

12 Since their establishment, during the British Mandate, the Rabbinical Courts have been accustomed to hear and rule on matters that are not within their jurisdiction under the Rabbinical Courts Jurisdiction Law, such as: tort law, property law, and monetary law in general. The Rabbinical Court relied on the Arbitration Law, which grants any person jurisdiction by virtue of the consent of the parties, subject to the signing of an arbitration deed. In 2006, the Supreme Court ruled that the rabbinical court was not authorized by law to serve as an arbitrator. See, HCJ 8638/03 Amir v. The Great Rabbinical Court in Jerusalem, 61(1) PD 259 (2006).

13 See, for example, HCJ 465/89 Raskin v. Jerusalem Religious Council, 44(2) PD 673 (1990).

14 See, for example, HCJ 153/87 Shakdiel v. Minister of Religious Affairs, 42(2) PD 221 (1988).

15 For more on the constitutional history of Israel from its establishment to the early 1990s, see, Gideon Sapir, The Israeli Constitution – From Evolution to Revolution ch. 1 (2018). [hereinafter Sapir – The Israeli Constitution].

The compromise decision was only partially implemented. Over the years, the Knesset enacted a series of basic laws, but these basic laws mainly set the rules of the political game and hardly dealt with the realm of values and human rights. In the absence of a constitutional human rights bill, the court created alternative mechanisms for the protection of human rights.[16] However, despite its activist approach, the Court exercised a degree of restraint and refused to invalidate primary legislation that violates human rights as long as a constitutional human rights bill has not been enacted. Over the years, several attempts have been made to enshrine a human rights bill in a basic law, but these attempts have been unsuccessful and no breakthrough has been in sight.

The lack of a constitutional bill of rights limited to some extent the court's ability to intervene in the status quo arrangements. This is because even after it effectively canceled the threshold requirements, it still could not intervene in arrangements that were anchored in primary legislation. For example, when a petition was submitted to the Supreme Court by a couple who wished to marry without the need for a religious ceremony, the court showed understanding of the petitioners' complaint, but was forced to reject the petition, referring to the provision of the Rabbinical Courts Jurisdiction Law, which granted exclusivity to religious marriage ceremonies. The court explained that "when there is an explicit statutory provision of the Knesset, which leaves no room for any doubt, it must be followed, even if it is inconsistent with the principles of the Declaration of Independence."[17]

In 1992, a momentous event took place in Israel, or at least this is how the Israeli Supreme Court interpreted it *ex post factum*. The Knesset passed two basic laws dealing with human rights. These were the Basic Law: Human Dignity and Liberty, and the Basic Law: Freedom of Occupation (hereinafter: the New Basic Laws). Three years later, the Court ruled that with the enactment of the two new Basic Laws, a constitutional revolution had taken place in Israel, and that from then on, the Supreme Court is authorized to invalidate primary legislation if it believes that it contradicts the Basic Laws.[18] This ruling gave the Supreme Court additional power and enabled it to expand the scope of its intervention in arrangements in the field of religion and state. Indeed, the Basic Law: Human Dignity and Liberty includes a grandfather section that protects laws passed before the entry into force of the Basic Law from repeal – and one of the reasons for its inclusion in the law was the desire to

16 For more information, see *id.*

17 CivA450/70 Rogozinsky v. State of Israel, 26(1) PD 129,135 (1971) (opinion of Justice Berenson).

18 CivA6821/93 Mizrahi Bank v. Migdal, 49(4) PD 221 (1995).

shield existing arrangements in the field of religion-state relations. However, the application of the grandfather clause is limited. It does not provide protection to new legislation or to laws that unjustifiably infringe, in the court's opinion, the freedom of occupation, which is enshrined in a separate Basic Law, which does not include a grandfather clause.

Here is an example: Since the establishment of the State, frozen meat has been imported exclusively by the State, through the Government Trade Administration. The reason given for this was that the State of Israel is in a state of emergency and therefore the regular supply of basic consumer goods must be ensured, and speculation must be prevented. According to this arrangement, the State imported only kosher meat, on the grounds that this simplified the task. In 1992, the Government decided to privatize the field of meat imports. It was determined that from now on imports will be made through private and commercial entities only, without quotas and without the need for an import license. A committee of directors general was established to formulate ways to implement the decision. The committee submitted its recommendations and the government began discussing them but postponed their implementation until an unscheduled date. Meatrael – a company which sought to import meat to Israel – petitioned the High Court of Justice. The Court accepted the petition and ruled that subject to the government's authority to make a different decision, "the state must implement its said decisions within a reasonable time, the period of which we set at four months."[19]

The Shas Ultra-orthodox party, which was a partner in the coalition, expressed opposition to the granting of import licenses in an uncontrolled manner. Shas argued that granting approval for the import of non-kosher meat would violate the status quo in this matter, and would lead to a flood of non-kosher meat in the country, the price of which is cheaper than the price of kosher meat.[20] The government discussed the matter several times and finally decided to regulate the privatization of the meat import industry by way of legislation. Until the legislation is completed, the situation will remain the same.

Meatrael appealed to the High Court of Justice again.[21] The Court ruled that the reason for the change in the government's position is rooted in "religious considerations," and that these considerations are *Ultra Vires*. Therefore, the court accepted the petition and ordered the state to grant Meatrael import

19 HCJ 2015/91 The heirs of the late Jacob Falcon v. Government of Israel, Nevo Legal Database 878 (May. 25, 1993).

20 There were those who disagreed with Shas's claim that the change in policy constitutes a violation of the status quo.

21 HCJ 3872/93 Meatrael v. Prime Minister, 47(5) PD 485 (1993).

licenses. Justice Orr, who wrote the main opinion in the case, added that the refusal to grant import licenses violates Meatael's freedom of occupation, and noted that this violation would not meet the limitations clause (which establishes conditions for legitimizing an infringement of the right).[22]

If the frozen meat affair had arisen before the enactment of the Basic Law: Freedom of Occupation, the government could have overcome the court's decision by anchoring the government monopoly in primary legislation, or by adding a stipulation in the law that the granting of licenses for the import of meat is contingent on receiving kosher approval from the Rabbinate. However, after the enactment of the new Basic Laws, the Court acquired the power to invalidate primary legislation that in its opinion contradicts the provisions of these Basic Laws. Therefore, anchoring the existing arrangement in the law could no longer guarantee immunity from harm to this arrangement.

The Meatrael ruling sent the coalition into a frenzy. The Shas faction, which realized that the usual political tools would not help it in this case, turned its attention toward the Basic Law: Freedom of Occupation. Members of the other religious factions also woke up from their slumber and understood the damage that the Basic Law caused to their interests. The political crisis worsened, and the Basic Law was in danger. At this point, the Court president, Aharom Barak, entered the fray. Barak offered the political system a compromise, according to which the Basic Law will be amended and an 'override clause' will be added to it.[23] The override clause will determine that a law that violates the freedom of occupation, and does not meet the conditions of the limitation clause, will nevertheless be valid if it is passed by an absolute majority of Knesset members, and it explicitly states that it was enacted despite what is stated in the Basic Law: Freedom of Occupation. A law that meets the conditions of the override clause will remain in effect for a maximum of four years, and then it will expire. Barak's intervention in the political crisis was most likely motivated by his desire to defend basic law: freedom of occupation and the entire basic law enterprise. From his point of view, it would have been better to weaken the Basic Law: Freedom of Occupation a little than to endanger its very existence.

---

22 *Id.*, at paragraph 24 of his opinion: "It appears that legislation according to which the import of meat will be conditional on the condition that it is kosher is legislation that restricts the freedom of occupation, not in accordance with the limitation clause."

23 See, Aharon Barak, On *the Amendments to the Basic Law: Freedom of Occupation*, 2 Mishpat Umishmal 545 (1994) (Barak's letter to the Chairman of the Knesset Constitution, Law and Justice Committee, including comments to the proposed Basic Law: Freedom of Occupation (Amendment). As the editorial board of the journal notes, "Justice Barak's comments found an echo in the new version of the Basic Law", ibid.).

The government adopted Barak's compromise proposal, and in its wake the Knesset. Although some Knesset members expressed opposition to the proposed amendment, arguing that it was equivalent to canceling the constitutional nature of the Basic Law, most Knesset members supported the proposal, either because they hoped that its adoption would restore political calm, or because they agreed with Barak's opinion that it was better to sacrifice one's "pawn" in order to save the "Queen". Following the amendment of the Basic Law, the Knesset enacted the Frozen Meat Import Law, 5754–1994. The law – which was passed by an absolute majority of the Knesset members and stated that it is valid despite what is stated in the Basic Law – stipulates that "a person shall not import meat unless he has received a kosher certificate for it [from the rabbinate]."[24]

The court's decision on the import of frozen meat was just one of a series of rulings handed down since the Constitutional Revolution, which constituted Court interventions in the status quo. The Court also intervened in the field of the sale of pork. By law, a local authority is empowered to enact a bylaw that will prohibit or restrict the sale of pork within its jurisdiction.[25] For years, many authorities enacted such bylaws, and the Court did not intervene in their discretion, but in 1999 the Court, headed by President Barak, ruled that because these bylaws infringe on freedom of occupation, limitations should be set on the extent of the restriction on the sale of pork that they may impose.[26] The court's decision necessitated the amendment of many bylaws, the contents of which were inconsistent with the precedent set by the court.

The Court has based its increasing involvement in matters of religion and state not only on the right to freedom of occupation. It has used a variety of values and rights to intervene in the decisions of the political system on these matters. This activity has marked the Court in general and the leader of the trend, Aharon Barak, as enemies of the ultra-orthodox camp and, to a certain extent, of the national-religious camp as well.[27] The frustration among the observant camp with the court's conduct was particularly manifested in a

24 Section 2 of the Law. Later, the name of the Law was changed, and today it is called the Meat and its Products Law, 5754–1994, SH 104.

25 Local Authorities (Special Authorization) Law, 5717–1956, SH 211.

26 HCJ 953/01 Solodkin v. Beit Shemesh Municipality, 58(5) PD 595 (2003). For a review and evaluation of the developments in the field of pigs from the beginning of the new settlement in Israel to the Solodkin case, see Daphne Barak-Erez, Outlawed Pigs: Law, Religion and Culture in Israel (2007).

27 For a review of the attack on the Supreme Court by religious and ultra-orthodox society, see Asher Cohen & Bernard Susser, Israel and the politics of Jewish identity: The secular-religious impasse 85–86, 90–91 (2000).

demonstration that took place in February 1999 in front of the Supreme Court building. At the demonstration, which was attended by between 250,000 and 400,000 people, harsh words were made against the court.[28]

2 A (Somewhat) Awakening of the Public Discourse

Alongside the gradual erosion of the status quo that took place during the 1980s and 1990s, this period experienced a certain revival of public engagement with the subject, especially in the following two issues: the status of the Sabbath and the enlistment of yeshiva students. Two main factors contributed to the growing preoccupation with the issue of conscription of yeshiva students: the significant increase in the number of young people who received exemptions, a fact that focused attention on the issue and increased public criticism. and the 1998 judgment, described above, in which the High Court of Justice invalidated the legal anchor on which the exemption arrangement was based, which obliged the political system to reexamine the issue.

The revival of the public discourse on the Sabbath has been advanced by two main factors. The first is the reservations of public figures and intellectuals – including opponents of legislation for religious reasons – about the gradual change that has taken place in the nature of the public Sabbath in Israel, which was expressed in the opening of many shopping centers, convenience stores, and movie theaters throughout the country.

The second catalyst for the growing public engagement with the Sabbath was the rift between the religious and the secular, which began to widen during the 1980s, with the collapse of the consociational politics on matters of religion and state.[29] The social rift worsened in the 1990s–in part because of the peace process promoted by the government of Yitzhak Rabin – and reached its

---

28 For a discussion of the demonstration and its significance, see Ran Hirschl, *The Political Origins of Judicial Empowerment Through Constitutionalization: Lessons from Four Constitutional Revolutions*, 25 Law & Social Inquiry 91, 122–123 (2000).

29 For a discussion of possible reasons for this change, see, for example, Asher Cohen, *Amanot le-Hasdarat Yachasei Chilonim ve-Datiyim – Nisyonot Hasdara Tziburiyim le-Nochach Kishalon Politi* [*Covenants for Regulating Secular-Religious Relations – Public Regulation Attempts in the Face of Political Failure*], *in* Shabat Achim – Yachasei Chilonim-Datiyim: Amadot, Hatza'ot, Amanot [A Gathering of Brothers – Secular-Religious Relations: Positions, Proposals, Covenants] 365 (Uri Dromi ed., 2005); Cohen & Zisser, Mehashlama Lehaslama, *supra* note 53.

peak in late 1995, when Rabin was assassinated by a kippah-wearer.[30] Various elements in the Israeli public felt an urgent need to act to mend the rift and established frameworks for discussing the controversial questions in order to try to find a common denominator.[31] Naturally, matters of religion and state in general, and the issue of the Sabbath in particular, were the focus of these discussions.

---

30 See, for example, Aviezer Ravitzky, *Let us search our Path': Religious Zionism after the Assassination, in* The Assassination of Yitzhak Rabin 141–162 (Yoram Peri ed.,2000).

31 For a review and evaluation of various treaties, see, Zvi Tzameret, *Amanot Chevratiyot Bein Chilonim le-Datiyim* [*Social Covenants Between Secular and Religious People*], *in* Covenants in Israel : attempts to regulate relations between the secular and the religious (2005); Asher Cohen, *Reshit Tznichet Ge'ulatenu – ha-Tzionut ha-Datit u-Netishat ha-Ma'avak al Zehutah shel ha-Medinah* [*The Beginning of the Decline of Our Redemption – Religious Zionism and the Abandonment of the Struggle for the Identity of the State*], *in* The Religious Zionism: An Era of Changes 364–385 (2004). [hereinafter Cohen, *The Beginning of the Decline*].

CHAPTER 4

From the Beginning of the 21st Century to the Present

The period between the beginning of the 21st century and the present is characterized by two trends: the secularization of the public sphere and the change in the focus of controversy on matters of religion and state. True, even before the establishment of the State of Israel, the field of religion-state relations was characterized by a gap between the law in the book and the law on the ground, but in recent decades this gap has been growing. At the same time, issues that were once the focus of public debate are losing their centrality, and new dilemmas are emerging, mainly relating to the state's relations with the ultra-orthodox public. This chapter will be devoted to describing the changes and the causes of their formation.

1 Secularization of the Public Sphere

In the literature, it is customary to distinguish between two perspectives for describing the legal situation: the law in the book – acts, regulations and court rulings, and the law in the field – the way the public behaves, in practice. An example that is usually given in this context relates to the speed limit. If the law sets a speed limit of up to 100 kilometers per hour but in practice the police does not act against those who drive at a higher speed, unless they have crossed the limit of 115 kilometers per hour, this means that from the perspective of the law in the field, the maximum speed limit is 115 km/h. In light of the above, it seems that a description of the situation in Israel in matters of religion and state cannot suffice with presenting the law in the book but must also be accompanied by a description of the actual reality. Indeed, an examination of the situation on the ground and its comparison with the law in the book reveals a considerable gap between the two.

The gap between the law in the book and the law on the ground in matters of religion and state has always existed in Israel. However, in recent decades it has been widening. A study conducted in 2014[1] sought to examine the content

1 Gideon Zeira et al, Achifat ha-Hora'ot be-Davar Ptichat Asakim ve-Sgiratam be-Yemei ha-Menucha al-Yedei ha-Rashuyot ha-Mekomiyot [Enforcement of the Provisions Concerning

© GIDEON SAPIR, 2026 | DOI:10.1163/9789004758889_006

of the bylaws relating to the closure of businesses on Shabbat and the extent to which they are enforced. The study surveyed 35 local authorities: 25 municipalities and ten regional councils. Only two of the municipalities did not have a bylaw regulating the opening and closing of businesses (2%). Eight of the regional councils had no such laws (80%). The bylaws generally refer to three categories: a dining hall (restaurants, cafes, etc.), a cultural facility (theaters, cinemas, museums, etc.), and a business (businesses that are not restaurants or cultural facilities). In most municipalities, the operation of eateries is permitted on Shabbat and Jewish holidays. The arrangements regarding cultural facilities are varied: in some authorities it is forbidden to open them on rest days, and in other authorities there are restrictions on the manner in which cultural facilities are opened or on the opening of certain types of these facilities. In most cases, it is forbidden to open businesses on rest days.

As for enforcement, the study found that out of the 25 authorities that have a bylaw, 13 do not fully enforce it. Fifteen of the authorities examined reported that they did not have information on the rate of businesses open on rest days in their jurisdiction.

A study conducted by the Institute for Zionist Strategy in 2015 examined the scope of activities that take place on the Sabbath according to a segmentation of areas and regions. In the context of this topic, the data regarding activity in malls and shopping centers are particularly interesting. The study found that 20% of malls and shopping centers operate on Shabbat (39 out of 196). A breakdown by district shows that the Tel Aviv district is the most prominent district in terms of commercial activity on Shabbat, while the Jerusalem district is the district with the lowest rate of activity on Shabbat: 29% of malls and shopping centers in the Tel Aviv district operate on Shabbat (9 out of 31) compared to 0% in the Jerusalem district (0 out of 15).[2]

What can explain the growing gap between the law in the book and the law on the ground? Guy Ben-Porat believes that the reasons for the secularization of the public sphere in Israel in recent years are mainly economic rather than ideological. The secular ideological struggle in the political arena is gradually being replaced by personal choices that shape the public sphere in practice. Ben-Porat attributes the expansion of commercial activity on the Sabbath to the rise of consumer culture in Israel.[3] This explanation is plausible, but it is

---

the Opening and Closing of Businesses on Days of Rest by the Local Authorities] (Knesset Research & Info. Ctr. 2014).

2 Ariel Finkelstein, Sabbath in Israel : the full picture 4–6 (The Inst. for Zionist Strategy 2016).

3 Guy Ben-Porat, Between State and Synagogue: The Secularization of Modern Israel (2013). [hereinafter Ben-Porat, The Secularization of Nodern Israel].

incomplete. It explains the changes in attitudes and preferences among the public, but it does not explain why the relevant governmental bodies refrain from enforcing the law as it appears in the book. This may be due to a change in the political agenda of the religious sector. Let's take the issue of the Sabbath as an example. In the first four decades of the state's existence, the struggle to restrict commerce and work on the Sabbath was led by Knesset members from the party representing religious Zionism. Since the 1990s, there has been a change in the attitude of representatives of that sector to the issue of the Sabbath and to questions relating to the relationship between religion and state in general. The change is expressed in two ways: in the lack of engagement with these issues among representatives of the sectoral party,[4] and in contrast, the attempts of national-religious Knesset members who are not members of the sectoral party to promote reforms on the same issues.

The aforementioned change can be explained in various ways. Menachem Mautner argues that among religious Zionist leadership, there was a willingness in the relevant years to cooperate intellectually, socially, and politically with the secular public, based on an egalitarian attitude and recognition of the cultural value of the secular public.[5] If Mautner is right, this could provide a reason for the weakening of the National-Religious public's insistence on religious legislation in general, and in particular in the area of the Sabbath. Another possible explanation may be based on the concentration of the National-Religious effort on the settlement front and the political-security struggle, which requires lowering the profile on other fronts, including matters of religion and state.[6] A third explanation will attribute the change to the trend of residential segregation that characterizes the national-religious public in recent decades, which weakens its interest in shaping the country' public sphere.[7]

The change in trend among religious Zionist politicians has sometimes skipped their counterparts in the ultra-orthodox parties. During the tenure of Eli Yishai of Shas as Minister of Labor and Social Affairs, he used his authority in charge of enforcing the Hours of Work and Rest Law and sent inspectors to shopping centers throughout the country that are open on the Sabbath,

4 See, Cohen, *The Beginning of the Decline*, *supra* note 82.

5 See, for example, Menachem Mautner, *The 1990s: Years of Reconciliation?* 26 Tel Aviv University Law Review 887 (2003).

6 See, for example, Cohen, *The Beginning of the Decline*, *supra* note 82.

7 Another geographical fact that has weakened the religious interest in the war against opening businesses on the Sabbath is that a large part of the shopping centers that have opened on the Sabbath in recent decades are located in open areas outside the cities, or at least outside the residential areas.

who imposed fines on business owners who employed Jews on the Sabbath without a permit.[8] Yishai expressed his opposition to any compromise that was proposed, and rebuked Knesset members from the religious-zionist sector, who, according to him, have become "reformists" on matters related to the Sabbath.[9] However, this brief episode is the exception. An examination of the activities of the Shas movement in recent decades in the field of public Sabbath observance shows that they, too, have significantly reduced their preoccupation with matters of observance of the Sabbath.

Support for this impression can be brought from the conduct of Shas leader Aryeh Deri on two issues: one relating to the municipal bylaw in Tel Aviv and the other to soccer games on the Sabbath. On the first issue, Deri, in his capacity as Minister of the Interior, was required to address the amendment made by the Tel Aviv Municipal Council to the municipal bylaw, while significantly expanding the scope of commercial activity permitted on the Sabbath. Deri 'dragged his feet' and for a long time refrained from referring to the amendment – to approve or disqualify it. Only at the last minute, after the Court ruled that the failure to address the amendment was equivalent to the decision to disqualify it, and invalidated this decision, Deri remembered to send a letter with reasons for the invalidation of the bylaw.[10] On the second issue, the soccer players' association petitioned the Tel Aviv Regional Labor Court against the decision of the National Football League administration to hold national league games on Saturdays, and to oblige soccer players to work on Shabbat, in violation of the provisions of the Hours of Work and Rest Law.[11] In response, the administration informed the court that it had applied to the relevant Ministerial Committee to grant a general permit for the weekly rest employment of all types of workers in the soccer industry, in accordance with the provisions of Section 12 of the Hours of Work and Rest Law. Deri, who served as Minister of Economy at the time, who is legally responsible for granting work permits on the Sabbath, did not accede to the request, but at the same time

8 Ben-Porat, The Secularization of Modern Israel, *supra* note 85.

9 *Id.*, at 195–196. However, it should be noted that the scope of the inspectors' activity was rather limited, allowing many business owners to evade supervision. See, Shlomit Levy, *Ha-Shabbat ha-Pratit ve-ha-Tziburit be-Yisrael* [*The Private and Public Shabbat in Israel*], *in* Sabbath – Idea, History, Reality 123 (Yaakov Blidstein ed., 2004).

10 Deri's letter is quoted in FH HCJ 3660/17 The General Association of Merchants and Self-Employed v. Minister of the Interior, Nevo Legal Database, para. 5 of President Naor's opinion Oct. 26, 2017).

11 SD (TA) 36537-08-15 The New Histadrut Clalit v. Football Leagues Administration – National League, Nevo Legal Database (Aug. 8, 2015).

he refused to accept responsibility for his refusal and refrained from using his authority and imposing administrative fines on violators of the law.[12]

2 Changing the Focus of the Dispute

2.1 *Introduction*

In the previous section, we pointed out the widening gap between the law in the book and the law on the ground, in matters of religion and state. While the arrangements set forth in the law have hardly changed, the public sphere is undergoing a gradual process of "secularization." We attributed the change to two factors: the change in the public's preferences and the weakening of enforcement in this area, which stems, among other things, from the fact that representatives of the religious public in the Knesset have almost completely stopped fighting for the enforcement of the arrangements.

At the same time, it seems that public and political attention on matters of religion and state is gradually shifting its focus. If in the past the discourse and political struggle focused on matters relating to the public sphere and the right of secular Jews to be free from the yoke of some of the arrangements, in recent years the focus on these issues has diminished and the controversy has shifted to focusing on the state's relations with the ultra-orthodox public. It should be emphasized that the public and political discourse on "traditional" matters has not stopped. However, alongside this, other issues have become more pronounced, the common denominator of which is their engagement with the interface between the state and ultra-orthodox society.

Changing the focus of the discussion on matters of religion and state requires explanation. We will first try to explain the relative weakening of the discourse on classical issues, and then we will offer explanations for the growing focus on issues relating to the state's relations with the ultra-orthodox sector.

2.2 *Reasons for the Weakening of the Engagement with Classical Issues*

As noted, in recent years, the public debate on classical issues has lost some of its intensity and frequency. A number of factors have contributed to this. The first reason is that over the years, ways have been found to soften the tension between religious requirements, which were anchored in legal arrangements, and the interest of the public that sought to be freed from their yoke. In certain

---

12 Administrative Offenses Regulations (Administrative Fine – Work and Rest Hours), 5750–1990, KT 1352, impose a fixed administrative fine on anyone who violates the provisions of Sections 9 and 9-A of the Hours of Work and Rest Law.

matters, it was the court that found a way around the problem. Thus, for example, the court moderated the problems involved in the religious monopoly on marriage in Israel, when it de facto recognized civil marriages that took place abroad, a recognition that also became de jure recognition two decades ago. As we noted above, this solution is not satisfactory from a human rights point of view, but its existence reduces the urgency felt by those who oppose the religious monopoly to fight for its change. In other matters, the bypass is created by other parties. Thus, for example, in the field of public transportation on Shabbat: Although official public transportation does not yet operate on Shabbat, in the past decade several semi-private mass transit projects have been established whose operation does not conflict with the provisions of the law, and they are filling the place of public transportation while it does not operate.[13]

Another factor that helped soften the tension in these matters was the authorities' failure to enforce the provisions of the law. For example, in recent decades, the prohibitions imposed by law on work and commerce on the Sabbath have not been enforced, and commerce and cultural activity on the Sabbath are flourishing. In these circumstances, there is less urgency on the side opposing these laws to try to change them. On the religious side, too, no special effort has been made to try to narrow the gap between the law in the book and the law on the ground, and the result is that the issue of the Sabbath does not occupy a significant place in the public discourse on matters of religion and state.

Some will argue that the claim that the provisions of the law are not enforced is inaccurate, as is the claim that the religious do not make an effort to enforce them. As evidence of their position, they will point to, for example, the two struggles mentioned above, one regarding the non-enforcement of the municipal bylaw in Tel Aviv that prohibited the opening of supermarkets on the Sabbath, and the petition of soccer players in the National League against their employment on the Sabbath without a permit. In both cases, the court accepted the petitioners' position; The High Court of Justice ordered the municipality to effectively enforce the ban on opening supermarkets on the Sabbath (a ruling that encouraged the municipality to amend the bylaw), and the Regional Labor Court prohibited the holding of soccer games on the

13 Currently, there are two types of transportation services on Shabbat that "bypass" the law's requirement to obtain a license as a condition for operating public transportation lines: "cooperative societies" – which define passengers on the lines they operate as members of an association, who are required to pay a symbolic sum in order to join it; and free lines, operated by a number of local authorities in the central region.

Sabbath. However, further study shows that these two examples not only do not refute the claims, but in fact they strengthen them. First, in both cases, those who started the struggle and complained about the lack of enforcement of the law were not the religious, but rather people who at most can be called "traditional" and who also did not represent political actors. Second, in both cases, the attempt to enforce the law led to a change for the worse from the perspective of the petitioners. In the first case, the Tel Aviv Municipality amended the bylaw, significantly softening of the prohibition on opening businesses on the Sabbath, and an examination of the reality shows that the municipality does not enforce even these softened new restrictions.[14] In the case of the soccer players, the matter ended with the state granting a sweeping permit to employ the players on the Sabbath.[15]

2.3 *The Causes of the Increased Discourse in State-Haredi Relations*

2.3.1 The Demographic Change

As of 2021, the ultra-orthodox community in Israel numbered just over a million people, constituting about 13% of the country's citizens.[16] Although this is a relatively small group, about one-eighth of the country's citizens, the Haredi growth rate is 4% per year, and it is the fastest in Israel. According to the forecast of the Central Bureau of Statistics, in 2033 more than two million Haredim will live in Israel, and in 2065 Haredim will be about one-third of the country's citizens.[17] Haredi society is composed of three main streams: Hasidim, Lithuanians, and Mizrahim (Sephardim). There are differences between these three streams that derive, among other things, from the adoption of a different halakhic tradition and the different nature of the spiritual and political leadership of each of them.[18]

In contrast to the ultra-orthodox communities living outside of Israel, in which many members of the community integrate into the general labor market after their marriage, in Israel the leaders of the Lithuanian ultra-orthodox

14 For more information, see, David Aronovsky & Gideon Sapir The Story of Shabbat 225–249 (2022).

15 See, Dor Bloch, *Yesh Ishur: Hushag Heter le-Mischakei Kaduregel be-Shabbat* [*There is a Permit: A Permit for Soccer Games on Shabbat Has Been Obtained*], Sport 5 (Feb. 20, 2018), https://www.sport5.co.il/articles.aspx?FolderID=64&docID=270303.

16 Lee Cohener & Gilad Malach, Statistical Report on Ultra-orthodox Society in Israel (Isr. Democracy Inst., 2021).

17 The Central Bureau of Statistics, Religion and Self-Definition of Religiosity, The Face of Israeli Society 66 (Report No. 10 2018).

18 For more information, see, Haim Zicherman, Black, Blue and White: A Journey into Charedi Society in Israel (2014).

stream have introduced the "Society of Learners" which directs ultra-orthodox men to continue their religious studies after their marriage, without a date of completion, while relying financially on subsistence scholarships and the wages earned by their wives who go to work. The society of learners developed through the establishment of an extensive network of kollels (daily Torah institutions for married ultra-orthodox Jews), funded partly by the state and partly by private donors. The success of the society of learners model has led to the fact that many Haredi men do not work but study in a kollel, and as a result, many Haredi families live in poverty and deprivation. Over the years, the Lithuanian society of learners model spread to the other ultra-orthodox sub-communities – the Chassidim and the Sephardim.

In the first decades of the state's existence, ultra-orthodox society was relatively small. Most of the ultra-orthodox public lived in mixed localities (religious and secular). Many of the ultra-orthodox worked for a living, and some even enlisted in the army. Beginning in the 1970s, the ultra-orthodox began to converge on boundaries and exclude themselves from the Israeli public domain in many areas:

> *Housing* – In recent decades, separate ultra-orthodox cities and neighborhoods have been established, enabling the creation of a special character, which includes the closure of roads to vehicular traffic on Shabbat and Jewish holidays, and many public buildings, which serve educational and religious institutions.
>
> *Education* – Since the establishment of the State of Israel, there has been a non-state ultra-orthodox education stream, which is budgeted by the state, but controlled only to a limited extent, so that schools are able to introduce an agenda and curriculum with unique content. As of 2020, the ultra-orthodox education system constitutes about 20% of the education system in Israel.
>
> *Employment* – Haredi livelihood is significantly based on jobs within the community, some of which are Rabbinic jobs, some are in the education system, and some in other professions. About 100,000 married Haredi men are yeshiva students whose Torah is their profession, and they constitute about 50% of all Haredi men.
>
> *Shouldering the security burden* – Most of the ultra-orthodox do not serve in the army at all, and a minority do so in unique service tracks, with a strict separation between them and all non-ultra-orthodox soldiers.

With the entry of the ultra-orthodox parties into the coalition in 1977, the Israeli government began to act in a variety of ways that aided the process of seclusion of the ultra-orthodox. However, the lifestyle of the growing ultra-orthodox society affects Israeli society as a whole. In the third generation of the State of Israel, the Israeli public expects the ultra-orthodox community to make a significant change in its way of life, a change which will be expressed on two main areas: first, broadening horizons and general knowledge, followed by vocational studies, integration into the employment circle, and payment of direct taxes to the public coffers; The second is to share the security burden through military or civilian service.

The call for ultra-orthodox integration into the various circles of life in Israel does not fall on deaf ears. In recent years, there has been an upward trend in the percentage of Haredim seeking to acquire higher education. A small number of young ultra-orthodox men, smaller than necessary, even enlist in the army. The trend of integration stems not only from the internalization of public criticism, but is also influenced by the harsh economic reality that characterizes ultra-orthodox society and, to a certain extent, also from the exposure of the ultra-orthodox public to the increase in the average standard of living among the general public in Israel, an awareness that highlights the gap between them and the rest of the population. Another element worth mentioning in this context is the existence of initiatives, both governmental and private, that support the integration of the ultra-orthodox in the army, higher education, and the labor market, and establish infrastructures that enable integration.[19]

However, this trend of integration brings with it not only hopes, but also new challenges. The ultra-orthodox, who are interested in acquiring higher education or serving in the army, wish to do so while maintaining religious commandments, which (in their understanding) include, among other things, a demand for complete separation between the sexes, which requires the establishment of unique frameworks in which segregation will be maintained. This demand is not accepted with sympathy by some of the general public.

In the situation that has been created, both sides are faced with a dilemma. As for the general public: On the one hand, it demands that the ultra-orthodox public integrate and fulfill its share of the economic and security burden,

---

19 See, for example, Decision No. 869, 34th Gov't, Kidum Hamlatzot le-Shiluv ha-Ukhlusiyah ha-Charedit be-Sherut ha-Medinah [Advancing Recommendations for Integrating the Haredi Population in the Civil Service] (Dec. 20, 2015). Today, the IDF has many programs adapted to the Haredi population. For a review of academic frameworks adapted to Haredi society, see Dganit Levy, Shiluv Haredim be-Haskala ha-Gvoha [Integration of the Haredi in Higher Education] 27 (Jerusalem Inst. for Pol'y Rsch. 20212021). With regard to integration into employment, mention can be made of the KEMACH (Promoting Haredi Employment), which deals with the advancement and integration of the Haredi population into employment.

because maintaining the status quo becomes practically impossible and morally unacceptable. On the other hand, it finds it difficult to accept the price involved in integration, which will be expressed in a change in the nature of the public sphere, and perhaps, in its heart, it is contemplating whether it would not have been better for the ultra-orthodox to continue to seclude.[20] As for the ultra-orthodox public: On the one hand, many of them are beginning to take the first steps to integrate into the labor market and the army, whether for moral reasons or for utilitarian reasons. On the other hand, there are strong forces within the sector that warn against integration and claim that the real goal of the demand for integration – or at least the expected result of this integration – is to undermine the walls that have protected the ultra-orthodox from the temptations of secularism to this day.

Another factor that intensifies the tension in the state's relations with the ultra-orthodox is the numerical growth of ultra-orthodox society. Although most of the ultra-orthodox still live in separate cities and neighborhoods, the increase in numbers leads to the expansion of their sphere of living, which adds new points of friction. In this context, we can mention the controversy over the existence of gender-segregated cultural events, using public resources, as well as the controversy over gender segregation in public transportation. In recent decades, cities and neighborhoods have been established throughout the country that are intended for the ultra-orthodox public. Part of this public, most of whom travel by public transportation, seeks to adapt the reality of these transportation lines to the rules of modesty that are customary in the sector.

Finally, the trend of modernization in ultra-orthodox society also contributes to the tension, which also creates tensions that did not exist in the past. For example, the ultra-orthodox are increasingly listening to radio broadcasts and talking to each other on a cell phone, and in these areas as well, they are

---

20 For example, many employers refrain from employing Haredi workers, out of fear of the changes they will be forced to make in the business and the shared space. See, e.g., Neta Moshe, Mipui Chasamim ha-Omdim Bifnei Kidum Haredim be-Tafkid u-ve-Sachar ba-Avodah [Mapping Barriers to Promotion of Haredim in Job and Wages at Work] 8 (Knesset Research & Info. Ctr. 2016); GILAD Malach et al, A Master Plan for Ultra-Orthodox Employment in Israel 77 (Isr. Democracy Inst., Policy Paper No. 111, rev. ed 2016). Regarding military service, see, Elisheva Rossman, *Al Mah Anachnu Medabrim Ke-she-Anachnu Medabrim al Giyus Haredim le-Tzahal?* [*What Are We Talking About When We Talk About Haredi Enlistment in the IDF?*] ", Ma'aracot (May 22, 2024), https://www.maarachot.idf.il/29055. Especially under the title Ha-Im ha-Chevra ha-Yisraelit Rotza be-Emet she-Haredim Yitgayisu le-Tzahal? [Does Israeli Society Really Want Haredim to Enlist in the IDF?].

trying to adapt the new tools to their lifestyles. They seek to avoid putting women on the air and to minimize the danger that the use of the phone will lead to surfing websites and breaching the fence.[21] On the face of it, one could argue that this is an internal matter that the state has no way of intervening in, and perhaps there is no justification for it. But this assumption is wrong. Radio broadcasts involve the use of a public resource – the airwaves – and this allows the law enforcement system to intervene. The field of cellular communications, on the other hand, is regulated by legislation, and in order to adapt it to the needs of the ultra-orthodox community, it is necessary to turn to the legislature. In both cases, the ultra-orthodox encounter opposition to the realization of their wishes, while on the other hand, they exert political pressure to realize their aspirations.

2.3.2 The Change in the Political Map

In the previous chapter, we described how the loss of the hegemony of Mapai and its successor, the Labor party, turned the religious parties into a tipping point between the left-wing and right-wing blocs. Among the religious parties, the bargaining power of the ultra-orthodox is greater than that of the parties representing the national-religious sector. This is because the vast majority of the national-religious public holds a hawkish worldview in the security field, hence the option of joining forces with the left is irrelevant to them. For the ultra-orthodox, the situation is different. While there is also a clear right-wing inclination among the ultra-orthodox public on foreign affairs and security, the combination between the growing needs of this public and the tendency of most members of the sector to obey the instructions of its spiritual leaders allows its political representatives some flexibility when they come to the negotiating table.

Despite the above, the transformation of the ultra-orthodox into a tipping point is not self-evident, and one would have assumed that their bargaining power would diminish over the years. This is because the dispute between the left and the right is not limited to foreign affairs and security, but the bloc's affiliation also predicts well the position taken on matters of religion and tradition. The typical right-wing voter will usually be closer to tradition than his fellow left-wing voter. Ostensibly, one might have expected that the widening

21 The percentage of Haredim who own a smartphone is on the rise, but it is still a relatively low percentage of the entire Haredi community. In 2022, the percentage of those who own a smartphone was 36%, see, Eitan Regev & Yehudit Miletsky, Doch Matzav ha-Hevra ha-Haredit [The State of Haredi Society Report] 153 (The Inst. for Zionist Strategy & Haredi Policy 2023).

gap between the left and the right in relation to religion would also weaken the bargaining power of the ultra-orthodox, both because the spiritual leaders of this community will attach great importance to this issue and would prefer a partnership with the traditional right, and because the parties representing the left would listen to their voters and be reluctant to accede to the ultra-orthodox demands. However, interestingly, in practice, this issue still does not have a decisive effect on the bargaining power of the ultra-orthodox. Indeed, the ultra-orthodox parties tend to prefer the right-wing bloc. However, the leaders of the left-wing parties show great generosity toward the ultra-orthodox, despite the distance, not to mention disgust, that some of them feel toward the ultra-orthodox. Time and again, they offer the ultra-orthodox generous deals, if only they agree to join the left-wing bloc and help it form a government. In light of this interesting phenomenon, the option of joining the ultra-orthodox with the left is on the table and preserves their ability to defend the interests that are important to them.

CHAPTER 5

From Here Forward – the Challenges

1 Introduction

The increase in the relative share of the ultra-orthodox sector poses a serious challenge. The continued existence of an ever-increasing society of learners is becoming a burden that Israeli society finds difficult to bear. The current reality reinforces the feelings of frustration and anger among the general public in Israel, which feels that it is required to carry a double burden on its back. This reality requires us to look for ways to increase the share of the ultra-orthodox public in the labor market and in dealing with security threats. Here we encounter two challenges: The first challenge concerns the question of how to achieve the goal. The second challenge concerns the question of how to deal with the necessary changes, from the ultra-orthodox perspective, as a condition for their integration into the higher education system, the labor market, and the military – changes that a part of the general public fears or opposes accepting.

Moreover, even if it were not for the urgent need to integrate the ultra-orthodox into the army and the labor market, the growing dominance of the ultra-orthodox public and the certain modernization it is undergoing requires attention. Although the Haredi public tends to withdraw off, the changing reality increases its affinity for the general public sphere, and raises questions that did not exist in the past. There is a considerable gap between the norms accepted by the general public and the norms accepted by the Haredi public, and the question is whether and how it is possible to reach an agreed-upon solution regarding the management of the public space. The inclusion of Haredim in the public sphere of secular nature makes the challenge of living together more significant. This is because the ultra-orthodox public is unwilling and unable to accept the character of the general public sphere. To be accurate, this is not a new question, for there is also a certain gap between the secular norms and those of the National-Religious public, which does not confine itself in its own narrow sphere. However, this public tended, at least in the past, to come to terms more easily with the secular nature of the public sphere.

Below we will briefly describe a number of key issues relating to the relations between the state and the ultra-orthodox public, a description that will illustrate the challenges in this area. Later, we will draw the general boundaries within which the arrangements should be placed on the various issues and will

 | DOI:10.1163/9789004758889_007

point out appropriate political tools and moods that will improve the chances of a feasible solution.

In the margins of this discussion, we will briefly address an additional challenge that has been emerging in Israel in recent decades due to the State of Israel's immigration policy – the formation of a group of immigrants that does not belong to the Jewish collective. This challenge is not related to the relationship between the ultra-orthodox and the state, and to a large extent it does not relate to the relationship between religion and state, but rather to the question of the national identity of the state. However, at least in the past, it was customary to include certain aspects of the issue in the framework of the discussion of matters of religion and state, and therefore we have chosen to address it here in short.

2 Conscription

We described above how in 1998 the Supreme Court invalidated the exemption arrangement for yeshiva students after ruling that the Minister of Defense was not granted legal authority to decide the fate of all yeshiva students. The court suspended the validity of the decision in order to allow the political system to prepare an alternative arrangement and to enshrine it in primary legislation. Following this ruling, the government appointed a public committee to propose a proper arrangement. The committee recommended that yeshiva students be able to continue to receive an exemption from military service, but after four years of study, they would be able to leave the yeshiva for a "decision year" at the end of which each student would decide on his future: if he wished, he could return to study at the yeshiva and not enlist in the army, and if he wished to leave the yeshiva, he would be drafted for shortened military or civilian service, after which he would be free to continue with his life.[1] The Knesset adopted the committee's recommendations and anchored them in law.[2] The validity of the law was set at five years from the date of its publication, and the Knesset was given the authority to extend its validity for an additional five years.

1 Do"ch ha-Va'adah le-Gibush ha-Hesder ha-Ra'ui be-Noge'a le-Giyus Bachurei Yeshivot le-Tzahal [Report of the Committee for the Formulation of the Proper Arrangement Regarding the Enlistment of Yeshiva Students to the IDF] (2000).

2 Deferral of Service for Yeshiva Students Law, 5762–2002, SH 521.

Shortly after the law was enacted, a number of petitions were filed against it, and they were heard by an expanded panel of nine judges.[3] The petitioners argued that the law violates the right to equality, and that this violation does not meet the conditions of the limitation clause in the Basic Law: Human Dignity and Liberty. Since the petitions were based mainly on the claim of violation of equality, the court was first required to rule on a question that has not yet been decided: Is the right to equality enshrined in the new Basic Laws, even though it is not explicitly mentioned there, and was even deliberately omitted from the law? Most of the justices held that the right to equality is included in the constitutional right to human dignity enumerated in the Basic Law: human dignity and liberty, and that the arrangement established in the law violates this right, by discriminating between those who serve in the army according to the usual rules, and yeshiva students, who are entitled to exemption. After determining this, the court turned to the limitation clause to examine whether the infringement of the right could be justified.

President Barak, who wrote the main opinion in the case, determined that the Deferral of Service Law includes a number of worthy purposes, including support for Torah study – support based on recognition of the value of these studies and the uniqueness of Haredi society – and increasing equality in the distribution of the burden of military service in Israeli society – as opposed to the current situation, in which the vast majority of Haredim do not serve at all. From there, Barak continued to examine the question of proportionality of the law. His main argument was that the picture that emerged three years after the law came into effect did not match the expectations in terms of the purposes mentioned above. However, in light of the fact that this is a temporary order intended to examine processes over time, Barak decided not to make a decision on the matter and to wait until the end of the five-year period.

As noted, the validity of the Deferral of Service Law was limited to five years, but the Knesset was given the authority to extend this period, and it did use this authority to extend the law for another five years. Immediately afterwards, a number of petitions were filed with the High Court of Justice against the law.[4] The main question that preoccupied the court was whether the particular growth in the number of ultra-orthodox enlisting in the IDF and national service was the "significant change" demanded by the Supreme Court in the previous ruling.[5]

---

3 HCJ 6427/02 The Movement for Quality Government in Israel v. The Knesset, 61(1) PD 619 (2006).

4 HCJ 6298/07 Ressler v. Minister of Defense 65(3) PD 21 (2012).

5 *Id.*, at para. 6 of Justice Hayut's opinion.

In February 2012, a ruling was handed down in the case. The majority justices ruled that the data presented to the court did not establish a connection between the means set forth in the law and the declared goal of increasing equality. In light of this, it is not possible to justify the violation of equality embodied in the law, and therefore it should not be extended beyond its expected expiration date in August 2012.

In light of the High Court ruling, the Knesset established a special committee to formulate an agreed-upon arrangement. The new arrangement, from 2014, established a two-stage process for integrating yeshiva students into military and civilian service, which would span nine years.[6] The law set a minimum annual target for enlistees for military and civilian service, and required the government to increase this number every year. In the first stage, denoted the "first adjustment period," this will be a completely voluntary arrangement, with no element of coercion. During this period, yeshiva students will be able to choose whether to enlist or continue studying in yeshiva. In the second stage, denoted the "second adjustment period", the setting of the goals will have practical significance. During this period, it will be possible to postpone enlistment until the age of 21, regardless of the goals, but from this age a yeshiva student will be able to receive an additional enlistment postponement only if the enlistment goals of that year have been achieved. If they fail to do so, all yeshiva students – from the age of 21, with the exception of 1,800 outstanding yeshiva students – will be required to enlist for military or civilian service, and economic and criminal sanctions will be imposed on those who evade military service. The second adjustment period was set to end on June 30, 2023, but the law did not specify what would happen after that date.

A number of petitions were also filed against this arrangement, but before a ruling was handed down on the matter, the Knesset approved another amendment to the Defense Service Law, which softened the arrangement and allowed the Minister of Defense to continue granting an exemption from conscription during the second adjustment period, even if the conscription targets were not met.[7] Following the amendment, another petition was filed, and all the petitions were heard together. In September 2017, the court annulled the aforementioned arrangement, by a majority opinion, after finding two main flaws in

6 Defense Service Law (Amendment No. 19), 5774–2014, SH 350.

7 Defense Service Law (Amendment No. 21), 5775–2015, SH 262. Section 26–18(3) of the amended law stipulates that the minister may postpone the summoning of a candidate for enlistment in these circumstances, "taking into account the security needs and the scope of the regular forces," and that he will decide how many orders to postpone enlistment will be issued, "taking into account the overall annual target for enlistment."

it: "First, the fact that the new conscription arrangement also remains dependent exclusively on the goodwill of the executive branch and yeshiva students and the ultra-orthodox community, since it did not prescribe practical sanctions [...] The second lies in the temporariness of the new arrangement, and in the absence of an arrangement of a permanent solution on this matter."[8]

Since 2017, the Knesset has not yet passed a law regulating the issue of ultra-orthodox service in the army, despite attempts to do so. Ostensibly, in the absence of an anchor in the law that allows the continuation of the exemption, the army was supposed to enforce the obligation to enlist young people in the ultra-orthodox sector. However, the High Court of Justice has repeatedly rejected the entry into force of the judgment that canceled the unique arrangement regarding the ultra-orthodox public. This enabled the army to leave the status quo intact. In July 2023, the amendments to the Defense Service Law, which regulate the special status of yeshiva students, which were approved in advance as a temporary order, expired, and as a result, as of July 1, 2023, there is no legal ground for the release of yeshiva students from IDF service. On March 28, 2024, the High Court of Justice issued an interim injunction in the petition, requiring the government to stop funding yeshivot whose students do not enlist.[9] In June 2024, the High Court of Justice ruled that the Israeli government is obligated to enlist yeshiva students in the army. The decision also prohibits the transfer of support funds to yeshivot and kollel for students who have received an exemption.[10] In early August 2024, the military authorities sent initial summons to 900 young ultra-orthodox men of conscription age, but the move was not successful, with only 48 of the invitees showing up.[11]

8 HCJ 1877/14 The Movement for Quality Government in Israel v. The Knesset, Nevo Legal Database (Sep. 12, 2017).

9 HCJ 6198/23 The Movement for Quality Government in Israel and 391 Others v. Minister of Defense, Nevo Legal Database (Mar. 28, 2024).

10 HCJ 6198/23 The Movement for Quality Government in Israel and 391 Others v. Minister of Defense, Nevo Legal Database (Jun. 25, 2024).

11 See, for example, Yinon Shalom Yatah, *Rak 48 mi-Toch 900 Hityatzvu: Nechsefu Netunei ha-Giyus me-ha-Migzar ha-Haredi* [*Only 48 out of 900 Showed Up: Enlistment Data from the Haredi Sector Revealed*], I24NEWS (Aug. 6, 2024), https://www.i24news.tv/he/news/israel-at-war/artc-56c93ae8;" *Ha-Kishalon ha-Muchlat: Rak 48 Haredim Hityatzvu be-Lishkat ha-Giyus mi-Toch 900* [*The Absolute Failure: Only 48 Haredim Showed Up at the Recruitment Office out of 900*], MAARIV ONLINE (Aug. 6, 2024), https://www.maariv.co.il/breaking-news/Article-1122998.

3 Education

The Compulsory Education Law, 5719–1949, imposes a responsibility on the state to provide education to all children in Israel. At the same time, the law requires parents of children of school age to ensure that their children regularly attend a "recognized" school, defined in the law as an "official school" or "other school", which the Minister of Education has declared to be a "recognized school for the purposes of this law". The law allows parents to be exempted from this obligation in a number of ways, including if the child is studying in an institution that the Minister of Education has declared an 'exempt institution'.[12] The State Education Law, 5713–1953, which was enacted a few years later, regulates the authority of the Ministry of Education to determine in the regulations, arrangements and conditions for declaring schools as recognized schools, to include a basic curriculum in them, and to provide them with support from the state budget. The regulations that were established condition the recognition of the institution, as well as its budget, on various conditions, including the requirement to maintain a basic curriculum of 75% of the total hours of study in an official school.

The Basic Plan, also known as the "Core Curriculum," was set out in the Ministry of Education's Director General's Circulars. In one of the cases discussed by the High Court of Justice, the Court noted that the core curriculum was intended to achieve two main goals: one, to serve as a link between all the factions of the people and all its sectors by creating a common denominator and harmony between the various human strata of society; second, to provide every child in Israel with basic tools for coping with life and to realize the right to equal opportunities in the development of his personality and self, both in his childhood and in his adulthood.[13]

The ultra-orthodox educational institutions, both elementary and secondary, are some recognized educational institutions and some are exempt institutions. These institutions are characterized by gender segregation and a unique curriculum. In secondary education, there is a significant difference between the institutions intended for boys and those intended for girls. In most girls' high schools, the core curriculum is taught. In contrast, in the vast majority of secondary institutions intended for boys, i.e., the "small yeshivot" (ages 13–17), the curriculum includes in-depth engagement with Talmudic issues but

12 The exempt institutions are educational institutions, mainly Talmud Torah for boys in the ultra-orthodox elementary school.

13 HCJ 4805/07 The Center for Jewish Pluralism v. Ministry of Education, 62(4) PD 571, para. 31 (2008). [hereinafter HCJ – The Center for Jewish Pluralism].

neglects all other areas. The issue of state funding for Haredi educational institutions, as well as the issue of the study material taught in them, have been at the heart of the social, political and legal discourse in Israel for many years. Below we will describe the main rulings that dealt with these issues.

In 1999, the first petition was filed on the subject of the core plan.[14] The petitioners argued that by not yet establishing a basic curriculum for the recognized schools, the state is violating its obligation under State Education Law. The state replied that there is indeed a gap between the types of institutions with regard to the supervision of the implementation of the curricula, but not in the very existence of programs that include core studies, since the curriculum used in the official educational institutions also applies to the recognized institutions. Ultimately, the petition was rejected with short reasoning, noting the state's commitment to publish within 30 days a circular from the Director General that will include the basic plan that will apply to recognized institutions.

Even after the state's commitment, a core curriculum for the recognized educational institutions was not published, and as a result, the small yeshivot continued to enjoy pedagogical autonomy. Therefore, in 2002, the Association of Secondary School Teachers petitioned the High Court of Justice against the budgeting of these institutions, claiming that it was done in violation of the law.[15] The court granted the petition, granting a three-year extension to rectify the situation, and set the beginning of the 2007 school year (September 2007) as the date by which the obligation to include the core curriculum in recognized educational institutions (especially secondary institutions) in the ultra-orthodox sector will be implemented, as a condition for their recognition and continued funding by the state.

The 2007–2008 school year began without the core curriculum for secondary education being introduced in the recognized institutions in the ultra-orthodox sector. Therefore, the Center for Jewish Pluralism and the Secondary School Teachers' Association petitioned the High Court of Justice, requesting that it enforce the ruling in the matter of the teachers' union.[16] A few days before the judgment in the petition, the Knesset enacted by a large majority the "Unique Cultural Educational Institutions Law," which regulates the budgeting of yeshivas. Section 1 of the Unique Cultural Educational Institutions Law

14 HCJ 2751/99 Paritzky v. Minister of Education and Culture, Nevo Legal Database (Jan. 23, 2000).

15 HCJ 10296/02 Secondary School Teachers' Association v. Minister of Education, Culture and Sport 59(3) PD 224 (2004).

16 HCJ – The Center for Jewish Pluralism, *supra* note 116, at 121.

defines a "unique cultural educational institution" as a secondary educational institution (grades 9–12), in which the education provided derives from the lifestyle of the unique cultural group, which is "the group of the ultra-orthodox population whose students study religious studies in a yeshiva according to Jewish law; or another population group determined by the minister." The purpose of the law, according to the explanatory notes, is "to enable the existence of educational institutions of the ultra-orthodox population group and other population groups [...] and establishing a mechanism for their budgeting. This is in light of the recognition of the importance that must be attributed to the rights of certain population groups and the need to ensure proper educational conditions for those studying in the educational institutions of these groups."[17] The law also stipulates that a unique cultural educational institution will be funded at a rate of 60% of the state's funding unit for each student in the formal education system, even if these institutions do not include core studies in their curriculum. The result of the law and the regulations in its wake is that the small yeshivas, in which most members of the ultra-orthodox community study in secondary school, receive partial funding without being required to include core studies in their curriculum.

In the judgment handed down a few days after the law was enacted, the court harshly criticized the Ministry of Education's "foot-dragging" and its attempts to circumvent the ruling given in 2004. Justice Procaccia, who wrote the main opinion, noted that she intended to accept the petition and issue a final order instructing the Ministry of Education to act immediately for the implementation of the core curriculum in all secondary educational institutions in the ultra-orthodox sector and to instruct the Ministry of Education to refrain from providing government support to an educational institution that does not maintain the core curriculum. However, due to the legislative development described above, the court refrained from issuing a definitive order, while emphasizing that it does not take a position with respect to the new law.[18]

Sometime after the enactment of the Unique Cultural Educational Institutions Law, a petition was filed, challenging its constitutionality.[19] The petitioners argued that the law violates the right of members of the ultra-orthodox community to receive a proper education, as well as their right to dignity, equality, autonomy, and freedom of occupation. In addition, the petitioners argued that the public's right to equality is violated, since the small

17 Draft Bill for Unique Cultural Educational Institutions Law, 5768–2008, HH 239 350.

18 HCJ – The Center for Jewish Pluralism, *supra* note 116, at 121 para. 83.

19 HCJ 3752/10 Rubinstein v. The Knesset, Nevo Legal Database (Sep. 17, 2014).

yeshivot receive preferential treatment compared to other educational institutions in the country. The court rejected the petition by a majority. Most of the justices in the majority held that the petitioners did not prove that the law violates the human rights protected by the Basic Laws. The others held that even though a violation of a constitutional right had been proven, the violation met the requirements of the limitation clause.

Another reason, raised by some of the justices, is rooted in policy considerations. Justice Hendel explained that this is a petition that "asks the court to cancel a central component of the cultural identity of the minority. This is in contrast to the traditional role of a court that deals with constitutional matters – to protect the rights of the minority from the majority."[20] Hendel believed that in such a case, one should act with "the necessary caution against a paternalistic approach as a basis for criticism of one group toward another."[21]

The majority justices' reservations about intervention were also based on practical considerations. In Justice Amit's opinion: "Imposing educational content on the ultra-orthodox sector is impractical. On the contrary, any sign of coercion only reverses achievements that have already been achieved, leads to a "consolidation of the ranks" in the ultra-orthodox public, in the face of what it perceives as a threat to its way of life. Coercion of educational content may be perceived as patronage, and it is doubtful that it will succeed on the practical level."[22] As stated, the petition was rejected, and as a result, the curriculum in the small yeshivot continues to include only religious studies, while at the same time these educational institutions enjoy partial funding from the state.

4 Gender Segregation in Academia

For decades, the presence of the ultra-orthodox community in the ranks of academia was minimal. The opposition to academia stemmed from two main reasons: first, the nature of academic study – which includes questioning the basic concepts – gave academia an apocryphal image that is not suitable for God-fearing people. Second, the format of studying together for men and women is not suitable for the ultra-orthodox who advocate gender segregation. As a result, the ultra-orthodox who went to work usually did so without academic training, and this significantly harmed their earning potential.

20 *Id.*, at para. 7 of Justice Hendel's judgment.
21 *Id.*, at para. 19.
22 *Id.*, at para. 21 of Justice Amit's judgment.

Since the late 1990s, a trend of change began to emerge, which was expressed in the expansion of the demand for academic degrees among the ultra-orthodox public.[23] A number of factors have led to the change: a certain weakening of the ideal of a Learning Society; an academic degree has become a kind of prerequisite for employment in almost every field; the saturation reached in the field of teaching, to which most ultra-orthodox women have been referred for years, which necessitated professional diversity and expansion of the ultra-orthodox employment circles; the trend of "academization" led by the government, in which the requirement for an academic degree has been added to the occupation of many professions as a condition for working in the field.

Over the years, the number of Haredi students has increased, and the number of institutions offering study tracks for the Haredi public has also increased, and the fields of study on the various campuses have become more diverse. In parallel with the increase in demand for academic education among the Haredi public, academia has also undergone changes in recent decades. One of the most prominent of these is the increased competition between the institutions and the growth of colleges, both private and public, alongside universities. Activists from the Haredi population joined forces with some of the colleges and led to the creation of study tracks adapted for the Haredi population, with gender segregation.

In 2011, the Council for Higher Education formulated a multi-year plan with the goal of increasing the number of Haredim studying in academia, based on the understanding that the integration of Haredim into higher education is contingent on recognition of the unique characteristics of Haredi society and respect for its way of life.[24] The plan was criticized for various reasons – including the claim that it encourages the exclusion of women and raises concerns about the violation of equality – and a petition was even filed against it in the High Court of Justice,[25] but in light of the fact that this was a preliminary move, the court decided not to intervene, and made do with instructing the relevant parties to collect data for the purpose of formulating policy later on.

In May 2017, the Council for Higher Education published a draft of the second five-year plan, which was based on accompanying research and a survey of

---

23 See, Gilad Malach, A "Kosher" Degree: Academic Studies in the Haredi Sector 9 (2014).

24 HCJ 8010/16 Berzon v. State of Israel, Nevo Legal Database, para. 22 of the judgment of Justice Elron (Jul. 12. 2021) [hereinafter HCJ – Berzon].

25 HCJ 6667/14 Tirosh v. Council for Higher Education, Nevo Legal Database (Mar. 19, 2015).

attitudes, and after holding a written and oral public hearing.[26] The plan determined that continuing to make academia accessible to the ultra-orthodox population is a clear vital interest of the state and a basic condition for integration and success in the labor market. The findings of the study and the survey of attitudes showed that without gender segregation, between 70% and 80% of the ultra-orthodox public would refrain from studying in academia, and therefore it was determined that the 'principle of substantive equality of opportunity' requires the possibility of studying in separate frameworks. However, the Council for Higher Education determined that studying in separate tracks violates basic values and that gender segregation on campuses raises concerns about discrimination, both in the types of professions open to each of the sexes, and in the level of studies in institutions," and therefore "the right balance must be found" between the need to integrate the ultra-orthodox population and "the preservation of the right to gender equality and the absence of discrimination." In this spirit, the Second Five-Year Plan set a number of restrictions on the identity of the learners and on the study tracks: It was determined that only graduates of a unique cultural educational institution, as defined in the Unique Cultural Educational Institutions Law, or an institution with religious practices and an ultra-orthodox worldview, which is under the supervision of the Ministry of Education, will be allowed to study on these campuses. It was also determined that separate study tracks will be possible for undergraduate studies only.

A number of petitions were filed against the second five-year plan.[27] The petitioners argued, inter alia, that the implementation of the program violates the principle of equality. It was further argued that the segregation harms the ultra-orthodox student population, since if there were no separate institutions, many of them would study in the general institutions. The petitioners argued that the existence of separate campuses paves the way for the continuation of gender segregation within the community. Another argument of the petitioners was that a degree taught in gender and sectoral segregation, without exposure to the mosaic of Israeli opinions, is intrinsically deficient, and misses the goal of education at the base of academic institutions. On the other hand, a petition was filed, arguing that the restrictions imposed by the Council for Higher Education on the activities of the ultra-orthodox campuses infringe

26 Policy Decision, Council for Higher Educ., Mediniyut Rav Shnatit le-Shanim Tash'a'ch-Tash'p'b be-Nose Harchavat ha-Negishut shel ha-Haskala ha-Gvoha la-Ukhlusiya ha-Charedit [Multi-Year Policy for the Years 2017–2022 on the Subject of Expanding Access to Higher Education for the Haredi Population] (May 23, 2017).

27 HCJ – Berzon, *supra* note 127, at 132.

on institutional academic freedom and the right of ultra-orthodox students to study in accordance with their lifestyle and culture.[28] The petition specifically attacked the imposition of regulatory restrictions on academic institutions that are not funded by the state.

In its 2021 ruling, the court approved by a majority opinion the outline set out in the second five-year plan, and the continued existence of separate campuses for the ultra-orthodox. The majority justices ruled that opening the gates of academia to the ultra-orthodox population in order to integrate them into the labor market is a worthy purpose that the state must promote. It was also determined that although the activity of the campuses entails a violation of equality between women and men, this is a proportionate violation, and it must be accepted in the absence of any other, better option. At the same time, it was held that the exclusion of female lecturers from tracks in which men study constitutes prohibited discrimination and should be abolished immediately.

5 Gender Segregation in the Public Sphere

One of the most prominent characteristics of ultra-orthodox society is the commitment to modesty, which is expressed, among other things, in gender segregation at public events. Although the basis of gender segregation lies in a social and cultural perception, this perception has clear echoes in halakha, from the time of the Gemara to the sages of our time.

On the legal level, Section 3 of the Prohibition of Discrimination in Products and Services Law, Entry to Places of Entertainment and Public Places, 5761–2000, provides as follows:

> A person who is engaged in the provision of a public product or service or the operation of a public place shall not discriminate in the provision of the public product or service, in the provision of entry to the public place or in the provision of a service in the public place, on the basis of race, religion or religious group, nationality, country of origin, sex, sexual orientation, outlook, party affiliation, age, personal status, parenthood, or wearing the uniform of the security and rescue forces or wearing their emblems.

---

28 HCJ 8683/17 Kohelet Forum v. Council for Higher Education, Nevo Legal Database (Jan. 15, 2018).

However, within the framework of the exceptions to the law, it was determined that:

> Discrimination under this section is not considered – (3) in the existence of separate frameworks for men or women, where non-separation will prevent part of the public from providing the public product or service, entering the public place, or providing the service in the public place, provided that the separation is justified, taking into account, inter alia, the nature of the product, the public service or the public place, the degree of its vitality, the existence of a reasonable alternative to it, and the needs of the public that may be harmed by the segregation.

The interpretation of the scope of the exception is controversial. For example, there are those who believe that gender segregation in public transportation can be justified under certain conditions,[29] while others believe that gender segregation should not be accepted under any circumstances.[30]

Over the years, the practice of gender segregation in the public sphere has expanded. In this framework, segregation has been introduced in public transportation used by the ultra-orthodox population, as well as in a small part of the HMO branches located in ultra-orthodox areas. In the Mea Shearim neighborhood of Jerusalem, segregation has even spilled over into the streets during special periods of congestion, and thus one sidewalk was allocated for women and another for men. In light of these developments, various women's organizations have launched a struggle to reduce the phenomenon they called 'the exclusion of women in the public sphere'.

In one of the petitions on this issue, the separation of public transportation on the Mehadrin lines, which mainly serve the ultra-orthodox public, was discussed, according to which men sat in the front of the bus and women[31]

---

29 See, for example, Alon Harel & Aharon Shnerach, *Ha-Hafrada Bein ha-Minim ba-Tachbura ha-Tziburit* [*Separation between the Sexes in Public Transportation*], 3 Alei Mishpat 71 (2003); Shai Akavia Wosner, *Mehadrin o Madirin? Mabat Bikorti al Kavei ha-Mehadrin ve-Bagatz Regan* [*Excluded or Exclude? A Critical Look at the Mehadrin Lines and the Regan High Court*], *in* Guardians of the Walls: The High Court of Justice and the Ultra-orthodox Society 453 (Haim Zicherman & Gideon Sapir eds. 2023).

30 See, for example, Zvi Trigger, *Gender Segregation as Sexual Harassment*, 35 Tel Aviv University Law Review 703 (2013); Menachem Mautner, *Ha-Hafrada Bein ha-Minim ba-Merchav ha-Tziburi shel ha-Medinah ha-Liberalit* [*Separation of the Sexes in the Public Space of the Liberal State*], *in* Guardians of the Walls: The High Court of Justice and the Ultra-orthodox Society (Haim Zicherman & Gideon Sapir eds. 2023) [hereinafter Mautner, Separation between the sexes].

31 HCJ 746/07 Regan v. Ministry of Transport, 66(2) PD (2011).

in the back. In addition, the women traveling on these lines were required to dress modestly. The Petitioner argued that this arrangement discriminates and violates the dignity of women. The Court ruled that public transportation operators will be obligated to set up a sign on all bus lines in which 'Mehadrin Arrangements' have been operated in the past, a sign that will make it clear that every passenger is entitled to sit wherever he chooses. However, it was held that alongside the desire to ensure that seating arrangements on buses will be completely voluntary, flexibility should be allowed for those passengers who wish to drive gender segregation themselves. The court explained that "the guiding principle is that consideration of religious lifestyle is permissible, as long as it is not intended to impose the commandments of religion on another person."[32]

Following a number of events that included various aspects of segregation in funeral ceremonies, the government decided in late 2011 to establish an inter-ministerial team "to propose to the government ways to deal with the exclusion of women from the public sphere and to propose possible solutions to the phenomenon of the exclusion of women from the public sphere."[33] A week later, the Attorney General also appointed a team on the matter. In March 2013, the team submitted its conclusions to the Attorney General, and these were placed on the government's table about a year later.[34] The report's recommendations were that no gender segregation should be accepted in the public sphere, with a few exceptions that justify segregation, such as when it comes to a distinctly religious event.

Over the years, the Court have repeatedly addressed the question of gender segregation, and in the vast majority of cases, it has prohibited segregation. In one case, the declared policy of the ultra-orthodox radio station "Kol Barama" was discussed, "not to put women on the air on the various programs as broadcasters or even as random speakers." The Kolech Association – Religious Women's Forum, filed a motion to certify a class action against the radio station, claiming that the station's policy violates the prohibition on discrimination set forth in the law. The District Court approved the request and ruled that the radio station's policy constitutes illegal discrimination as well as a tort.[35] In addition, the District Court defined the injured group as "all the listeners of the Kol Barama radio station, as well as all the women who were interested

32 *Id.*, at para. 6, 11–12, 36–38 and 33 of the judgment of Justice Rubinstein.

33 4052 Government Decision (Dec. 29, 2011).

34 1526 Government Decision (Mar. 30, 2014).

35 CA (DC Jerusalem) 23955-08-12 Kolech v. Radio Kol Barama, Nevo Legal Database (Sep. 20, 2018) [hereinafter CA (DC Jerusalem) Kolech].

in listening to the station but refrained from doing so due to discrimination against women at the station, from the day the station began operating until the day the application to certify a class action was submitted."

According to the legal rule, a class action filed by an organization will be approved only if it is proven that there is difficulty in filing the claim by a plaintiff with a personal cause of action. An appeal filed by the station to the Supreme Court against the approval of the application – on the grounds that in the case at hand the condition was not fulfilled – was rejected.[36] The court ruled that the condition was fulfilled in the circumstances of the case, since "there is a reluctance on the part of ultra-orthodox women to stand at the forefront of the struggle to increase gender equality in the ultra-orthodox community due to their fear of harm to their status in the community." After approving the filing of the lawsuit, the District Court heard the claim on its merits, accepted it and awarded compensation in the amount of one million shekels for the benefit of the public. The court explained that this sum was based on the non-pecuniary damage suffered by the victims, and its purpose was to express the aversion to the phenomenon of discrimination against women, as well as creating deterrence against similar conduct in the future.[37]

In another case, the Afula Municipality's intention to hold a performance by Hasidic singers with gender segregation was discussed. Following a petition filed by the Women's Lobby, and against the background of the Afula Municipality's agreement that there was no room for gender segregation, the court ordered that the event be held without segregation.[38] Following this, the singer announced that the performance was canceled. At this point, a Knesset member from the Shas list filed an administrative petition on the matter. In the ruling, which was given a few hours before the start of the event, the court overturned the municipality's decision, which agreed to cancel the gender segregation.[39] The court ruled that the ultra-orthodox population has the right to benefit from public resources, in accordance with its lifestyle and culture, and that in the circumstances of the case, in the balance between the expected harm to the ultra-orthodox public and the harm to the secular public, the former has the upper hand. The court left it to the municipality to decide whether

---

36 LCivA 14/6897 Radio Kol Barama v. Kol Barama, Nevo Legal Database (Dec. 9, 2015).

37 CA (DC Jerusalem) Kolech, *supra* note 138, at para. 90 of the judgment of Judge Kanfi-Steinitz.

38 AdminC (DC Nazareth) 17029-08-19 Israel Women's Network v. Afula Municipality, Nevo Legal Database (Aug. 11, 2019).

39 AdminC (DC Nazareth) 23791-08-19 Arbel v. Afula Municipality, Nevo Legal Database (Aug. 14, 2019).

to hold the event separately, while recommending that it divide the venue into three parts, one for women, one for men, and another part without separation.

An appeal was filed against this decision to the Supreme Court, which was heard while the event was taking place.[40] The Supreme Court ruled that the trial court was not authorized to accept the petition in the first place, for procedural reasons, but since the incident was already underway, no operative relief was granted.

From the description presented thus far, it appears that the fundamental question of whether a public authority is permitted to hold an event for the ultra-orthodox public with gender segregation remains without an unequivocal judicial decision. On the other hand, the state's position, as expressed in the Attorney General's report and in the government's decision, holds that events in the public sphere should not be allowed to be held in segregation, and accordingly the Attorney General acts to prevent such events from taking place.

6 The Law of Return

The Law of Return, enacted in 1950, grants every Jew the right to immigrate to Israel, and together with the Citizenship Law, 5712–1952, it grants every immigrant the right to become a citizen of Israel. The Population Registry Law mandates the registration of thirteen entries in relation to each of the country's residents, including nationality and religion. Until 1970, the Law of Return did not include any definition of the term Jewish. This left a wide range of options. In 1970, the Law of Return and the Registry Law were amended. As part of the amendment, a definition of a Jew was added to the Law of Return – as the son of a Jewish mother or a person who converted, and the Registry Law refers to the provision in the Law of Return. From then on, the question ceased to be who is a Jew, and became – who is a convert, since the legislature did not determine which conversion would fulfill the requirement of the law. Over the years, the court intervened from time to time in government decisions on the matter, until in 2021 the court ruled that any conversion in a recognized Jewish community, in Israel or abroad, will be recognized for the purposes of the Law of Return and the Registry Law.[41]

As part of the amendment to the Law of Return in 1970, a section was added to the Law of Return, which was popularly known as the 'grandchild

40 AdminA 5435/19 Sharon v. Afula Municipality, Nevo Legal Database (Aug. 14, 2019).

41 HCJ 11013/05 Dahan v. Minister of the Interior, Nevo Legal Database (Mar. 1, 2021).

clause'. The scope of entitlement to return was expanded to include spouses of Jews, their children, grandchildren, and the spouses of these descendants.[42] Over the years, a kind of convention was created that the main motive for the dramatic expansion of the right to return was the broad definition given by the Nazis to Jews in the Nuremberg Laws. The definition of the Nazis also included those who had only Jewish roots. Recently, Netanel Fischer proved that this is a myth that has no basis in reality, and that this matter had no influence on the decision to add the grandchild clause.[43]

In the first decades, the challenges involved in the Law of Return focused on the question of who is a Jew or who is a convert. However, from the beginning of the 1990s onwards, the challenge has focused, to a large extent, on the implications of the grandchild clause.[44] The large waves of immigration from the countries of the former Soviet Union included a growing number of people entitled to return by virtue of the grandchild clause, and as a result, a large group of non-Jewish immigrants was created in Israel. In the first decade of the 2000s, there were fewer than 300,000 people, but today it is more than half a million.[45]

In the current reality, there are hundreds of thousands of citizens living in Israel who, according to the accepted definition among the Jewish public, are not considered Jews, but in practice they are part of the Jewish collective. They live within the Jewish public, most of them within family frameworks that include Jews, speak Hebrew, study in the state education system, and enlist in the IDF. Moreover, as time passes, the number of second-generation immigrants by virtue of the grandchild clause – those who were born in Israel or received most of their education here – is increasing.

The reality described presents us with a significant challenge. What should we do with this group of citizens? One option is to do nothing and hope that over the years the members of the group will gradually assimilate into the Jewish majority group. Some seek to strengthen this hope by pointing to the fact that throughout Jewish history The Jewish People have already experienced significant assimilation without conversion. Without expressing an

---

42 Section 4A of the Law of Return states that "the rights of a Jew under this Law and the rights of an immigrant under the Citizenship Law, 5712–1952, as well as the rights of an immigrant under any other legislation, are also granted to the child and grandchild of a Jew, to the spouse of a Jew and to the spouse of a child and grandchild of a Jew; To exclude a person who was a Jew and converted voluntarily."

43 See, Netanel Fischer, *Ha-Sipur she-Teram Supar al Chok ha-Shvut* [*The Untold Story of the Law of Return*], 26 HaShiloah (2022).

44 For further information, see Asher Cohen, Non-Jewish Jews in Israel (2007).

45 See, The Central Bureau of Statistics, press release (Dec. 28, 2023).

opinion on the practical feasibility of this hope, it is important to point out one major problem in relation to it: as long as the grandchild clause remains in place and as long as the State of Israel continues to serve as a desirable immigration destination for citizens of certain countries, the number of non-Jewish immigrants will continue to increase, making it difficult for them to integrate into the Jewish majority group.

Another option is to work vigorously for the conversion of non-Jewish immigrants, and to focus on women of childbearing age. Here we are faced with an obstacle in the form of those who hold a strict halakhic position on the question of conversion, and therefore demands are directed at the Orthodox establishment to adopt a lenient policy in the field of conversion. However, in this path as well, the continued existence of the grandchild clause stands as an obstacle. In recent years, the number of non-Jewish immigrants has exceeded the number of Jewish immigrants. Against the background of these figures, even those who hold lenient approaches may wonder what is the point of conversion efforts, when at the same time more and more non-Jewish immigrants are immigrating to Israel, some of whom are also completely disconnected from the Jewish cultural world.

To complete the picture in the demographic context, it is worth mentioning another growing phenomenon of migrant workers from third world countries. In recent decades, many migrant workers who have no connection to the Jewish people and have no interest in joining it have entered Israel and become citizens or permanent residents – with legal or illegal status. Members of this group also already have second-generation members who were born in Israel and are studying in the Israeli education system.

Among the Jewish public in Israel, there are those who do not see a problem with the developments described. In their view, the immigration of non-Jews to Israel diversifies the human capital in the country and weakens the Jewish religion's grip on the systems of government, changes that they welcome. This is a legitimate position, but it contradicts the basic definition of the State of Israel as the Jewish nation-state, and it is incompatible with the views and aspirations of the vast majority of the Jewish people living in the country. The tension between the basic definition of the state as a Jewish state and the emerging reality of a growing group of non-Jews immigrating to Israel and settling there – whether by virtue of the Law of Return or in other forms – therefore poses a significant challenge.

CHAPTER 6

So What Do We Do?

In the previous chapter, a number of challenges were presented relating to the relations between the majority group and the ultra-orthodox minority. In this chapter I will offer a number of general insights regarding the way in which it is worthwhile, in my opinion, to take steps to bring about the fair integration of the ultra-orthodox public into the various circles of life in the State of Israel.

- The ultra-orthodox must internalize and understand that whether they identify with the Zionist enterprise or not, every citizen of the state must contribute his or her part in the economic and security fields, and the ultra-orthodox cannot exempt themselves from this obligation. In a reality in which the rest of the citizens are groaning under the growing economic burden and are required to dedicate several years of their lives to defending the country, often at the risk of their own lives, arguments such as "I do not identify with the state", "I am willing to live a life of poserty and I do not ask the state for anything" or "I contribute to the state through Torah study" lose their moral validity. Moreover, in a reality in which the demographic weight of the ultra-orthodox sector is becoming heavier and heavier, the continued existence of the current situation endangers the country's economic and security stability, and as a result, becomes dangerous.
- Respect and trust are two mindsets that will improve the chances of dialogue that will lead to an agreement. Unfortunately, the petitioners' position against segregation in the ultra-orthodox tracks in higher education shows a lack of respect and trust among those who demand that the ultra-orthodox integrate. The assumption that all that is required to bring the ultra-orthodox to change their position on matters of modesty is to prevent them from studying in segregation reflects a basic lack of trust in the sincerity of the ultra-orthodox and a lack of respect for them and their worldview.
- It is impossible to demand that the ultra-orthodox integrate and at the same time refuse to make the necessary adjustments so that they can do so without giving up their beliefs and lifestyle. Such a refusal raises the suspicion that behind the demand for integration is an intention to 'normalize' the ultra-orthodox and convert them against their religion. Anyone who calls on the ultra-orthodox to integrate into the labor market and contribute their part in the security effort must understand that such integration will require the relevant public systems to undergo certain adjustments, even if they are not to his liking. The same applies to the use of public space. The ultra-orthodox do not demand that the public sphere be conducted in

 | DOI:10.1163/9789004758889_008

accordance with their beliefs and lifestyles, but only that they be allowed to use it from time to time, even if this involves gender segregation. Placing their right to use the public space on condition that they give up their principles is unjustified.

- One of the proposed reasons for refusing to go too far for the Haredim regarding the use of shared space is that it is contrary to the basic value of equality, since it involves harming and objectifying women. The Haredim do indeed hold the view that there are inherent differences between men and women, and that differences in the roles assigned to each gender are derived from them. Those differences also explain the rules of modesty that the Haredim take upon themselves, which are different from what is customary in general society. However, they insist that gender segregation does not objectify women and does not attribute inferiority to them. Anyone who is willing to listen to the Haredim and believes in their sincerity should at least question the validity of the argument regarding the violation of equality. Anyone who does not believe in the sincerity of the Haredim is sinning against another basic value – the respect we should have for the beliefs of others.
- The latter point sharpens a certain similarity, and perhaps a little surprising, between some of the arrangements included in the status quo and the position that refuses to go far with regard to the use of public space. Some of the status quo arrangements – such as the arrangement in the field of marriage and divorce and the refraining from operating public transportation on Shabbat – imposed restrictions on religious grounds on citizens who opposed them. Similarly, the integration of the ultra-orthodox into the public sphere on condition that they accept the norms accepted by the general public means that they are obligated to behave contrary to their religious beliefs. Anyone who criticizes the arrangements of the first type may perhaps understand the problem involved in setting the aforementioned condition. Of course, the validity of the latter argument is contingent on the Haredim's use of the public sphere in accordance with their accepted rules of modesty will not entail coercion by anyone who disagrees with these rules – whether he belongs to the general public or is an ultra-orthodox who holds a different opinion.
- Another reason mentioned as a reason for refusing to allow the ultra-orthodox to use the public sphere in their own way is that this will open the door to a gradual takeover of the entire public sphere by the ultra-orthodox and their rules of conduct.[1] From time to time, there are apocalyptic predictions that

1 Another possible source for the refusal may be the hostile attitude of part of the general public toward the ultra-orthodox public. See, Madad ha-Kativut shel Pnima[The Polarization Index of Inside], pnima, https://pnimaisrael.com/%D7%9E%D7%93%D7%93%D7%94%D7%A7

one day, the ultra-orthodox (or the religious in general) will oblige every woman and girl to cover their heads with a scarf. These predictions are very similar to the danger that Justice Aharon Barak warned against: If only the members of a religious community were allowed to veto the broadcast on Shabbat of a program filmed on them, this would eventually lead to the television ceasing to broadcast on Shabbat.[2] They are also reminiscent of a gloomy forecast presented by Justice Cheshin, according to which the closure of a certain road to traffic on Shabbat will lead to the closure of all roads in Jerusalem on Shabbat, and there will be no going out and no one coming in.[3] However, while the hidden fears that gave rise to these scenarios should not be underestimated, the way to deal with these fears is not to give them decisive weight in policymaking.

- Even those who are not convinced by my argument that justice requires a certain flexibility toward the ultra-orthodox, and who hold the opinion that they should be firmly opposed, may at least agree that any arrangement that is determined regarding the ultra-orthodox will be applied equally with respect to other groups as well. If the obligation to serve in the army, or national service, is imposed on young people in the ultra-orthodox sector, this obligation should also be enforced on young people in the Arab sector. If the state denies allowances or other benefits to a young ultra-orthodox man who refuses to enlist or serve in any other way, the same sanction is supposed to be applied to other young people, Jews or Arabs, who refuse to contribute their share. If a local authority decides to prohibit gender-segregated events that the ultra-orthodox public wishes to hold in its public space, it must apply the same policy to similar events intended for other communities.
- Human history teaches that social changes often occur gradually and slowly. An attempt to carry out a revolution usually fails, and even when it succeeds, the price it exacts from the public that experienced the revolution is very heavy, sometimes heavier than the benefit that arises from the sharp change. Therefore, even if a change in the relations between the state and the ultra-orthodox is required, the chances of achieving it will increase if it is carried out slowly and gradually.[4]

%D7%99%D7%98%D7%95%D7%91/. (while only 2% of the ultra-orthodox said that they hate secular Jews, 38% of the secular respondents said that they hate the ultra-orthodox).

2 HCJ 1514/01 Gur Aryeh v. The Second Authority for Television and Radio,55(4) PD 267, para. 7 of the judgment of President Barak (2001).

3 HCJ 5016/96 Horev v. Minister of Transportation, 51(4) PD 1, paras. 23–24 of the judgment of Justice Cheshin (1997).

4 For a critique of the rate of Haredi integration, see, Daniel Statman, *Bimkom Mavo: ha-Vikuach al Reformot ba-Chevra ha-Haredit* [*Instead of an Introduction: The Debate on Reforms*

- Among the options on the table is using coercive means. Familiarity with Haredi society, as well as a sober observation of the game that has been played in recent decades between the state and the Haredim regarding military service, show that the use of coercive means, and even the mere threat of using such means, are more harmful than beneficial. Threats strengthen the extremist elements on the fringes of Haredi society, increase the separatist tendency among this sector and harm the efforts made by various elements in the ultra-orthodox community to promote integration processes in the various fields, and in the army in particular.[5]
- The events of the past years – the massacre of October 7, 2023, and the Iron Sword War, the end of which is not yet in sight – have sharpened the need, which already existed, for the ultra-orthodox to share the burden, and especially the security burden. However, here too, reason should be separated from emotion. The enlistment of the ultra-orthodox here and now will not bring back to the IDF the missing divisions that have been dismantled in recent decades and will not inject new blood into the whitewashed veins of the military system. What we have here is a considerable amount of cynicism and a lot of emotion that is completely understandable, but a bad consultant in decision-making. Therefore, the insight that the use of coercive means to try to recruit the ultra-orthodox is not recommended still holds.
- If the threat to use coercive measures, and all the more so their use, are not helpful in advancing the goal of integrating the ultra-orthodox, the use of incentives for this purpose may actually be effective. The cut in child allowances, which was implemented a few years ago, has led to a decline in the fertility rate among ultra-orthodox women,[6] and there is no reason to assume that a similar move in connection with military service will not lead to a similar result. It applies to negative incentives, and no less so to positive incentives, and there is a reason and justification for using them at least in the initial stages, even if they are used in an unequal manner, i.e. that they will be given only to the ultra-orthodox and not to ordinary citizens.

---

in Haredi Society], *in* Ultra-Orthodox Jews in the Public Space 11, 18–19 (Isr. Democracy Inst., Daniel Statman ed. 2024) [hereinafter Statman, *instead of an introduction*].

5 See, Joseph Miller, *Hachra'a o Interaktzia: Model le-Nihul ha-Konflikt Bein ha-Chevra ha-Haredit la-Tzibur ha-Klali, be-Tguva le-Prof. Dani Statman* [*Decision or Interaction as a Model for Managing the Conflict between the Ultra-orthodox Society and the General Public, in Response to Prof. Danny Statman*], *in* Ultra-Orthodox Jews in the Public Space 39, 45–46 (Isr. Democracy Inst., Daniel Statman ed. 2024).

6 See, for example, Esther Toledano et al, The Effect of Child Allowance on Fertility 15–18 (Nat'l Insurance Inst., Rsch. & Plan. Admin. 2009).

- In addition to the use of economic incentives, there is merit in employing means of public advocacy. While Haredi society makes considerable efforts to block itself to outside influences, and as a result, the level of exposure of the Haredi public to the media and social networks is lower than that of the general public, modern reality makes total disengagement impossible, and the same is true of Haredi society. Moreover, as we explained above, although separatist tendencies have increased among the ultra-orthodox public, the interfaces between the ultra-orthodox public and the general public have been growing stronger in recent decades, and this fact also has an impact on the extent to which ideas and information are transmitted from one side to the other. However, for advocacy to succeed, it must be formulated in the ultra-orthodox language and express genuine respect for its values.
- There are those who express support for judicial intervention in matters related to the relations between the state and the ultra-orthodox, more than in other matters. The argument raised in favor of the court's intervention in this area is that the court balances in its rulings the unfair bargaining power of the ultra-orthodox.[7] My opinion on this matter is different. Political agreements involve mutual concessions. Each side insists on accepting what is most important to it and concedes to the other side on matters that are less important to it. In this way, we get a precise reflection and balance of preferences within society. Intervention – and especially selective intervention – by the court in agreements reached in the political field undermines this balance. This is the case in general, as well as in matters of religion and state.[8]
- Even if for some reason, the above argument – against judicial intervention in the decisions of the political system in matters of religion and state – is not convincing, such intervention is undesirable for practical reasons. The

---

7 See, for example, Amichai Cohen, *Shoftim, Avrechim ve-Interesim: Nituach Piskei ha-Din shel Beit ha-Mishpat ha-Elyon be-Yachas le-Chevrat ha-Lomdim* [*Judges, Yeshiva Students and Interests: An Analysis of the Supreme Court's Judgments in Relation to the Society of Learners*], *in* Guardians of the Walls: The High Court of Justice and the Ultra-orthodox Society 53 (Haim Zicherman & Gideon Sapir eds. 2023).

8 See, Ron Shapira, *Divrei Yemei ha-Mahapekha ha-Shamanit: Agada Metzuyeret u-va Mavo, Achad Asar Prakim u-Musar Haskel* [*The Chronicles of the Shamanic Revolution: An Illustrated Legend with an Introduction, Eleven Chapters and the Morality of the Intellect*], *id.*, at 79; Ido Porat, *Ha-Anomalya shel Yachasei Beit ha-Mishpat ve-ha-Haredim be-Yisrael: Batei ha-Mishpat ke-Zira le-Bitul Tvi'ot Kvutzatiyot shel ha-Mi'ut ve-lo le-Kabbalatan* [*The Anomaly of the Relationship between the Court and the Ultra-orthodox in Israel: The Courts as an Arena for Canceling and Not Accepting Minority Group Claims*], *in* Ultra-Orthodox Jews in the Public Space 105 (Isr. Democracy Inst., Daniel Statman ed. 2024).

court's intervention undermines the confidence of the ultra-orthodox public in the judicial system in Israel and thus strengthens the separatist tendencies among this public. On the face of it, the ultra-orthodox, as a minority group, should have relied on the High Court of Justice and trusted it, since the High Court is the place where minorities are supposed to receive relief and protection. In practice, however, the ultra-orthodox are hostile to the Supreme Court and see it as a bitter enemy. The hostility and lack of trust that the ultra-orthodox community has toward the High Court of Justice stems from the prevailing feeling among this society that the Supreme Court does not understand its values and as a result harms them in its rulings.

- Judicial intervention also weakens the chances of reaching compromises in the political arena. As noted above, the chances of reaching a compromise depend, inter alia, on the creation of a relationship of trust between the parties to the negotiations. Knowing that an agreed compromise is not necessarily the last word, because it may be overturned by the court, causes each of the parties, and especially the ultra-orthodox side, to suspect the sincerity of the other side, and as a result, to hesitate to agree to the concessions required to achieve a compromise.
- There are those who are optimistic about the future of the relationship between the ultra-orthodox community and Israeli society and others who tend to be pessimistic. I choose to stand with the optimists and believe that if we take the path outlined above, the future will shine on us.

www.ingramcontent.com/pod-product-compliance
Lightning Source LLC
Chambersburg PA
CBHW031333230926
51848CB00001B/219
9789004758872